**WHAT PEOPLE
ARE SAYING ABOUT**

# SEEN

"At a time when teen suicidality, self-harm, depression, and anxiety are higher than ever, Seen is just the right gift at just the right time for just the right people. Using a gentle and compassionate voice, Will and Dr. Chinwé integrate science and faith in remarkable ways that will help you see, hear, and connect with young people in your life. Immerse yourself in the depth and simplicity of this book, and you can become even better at giving youth the love and grace they so desperately need."

—JOHN SOMMERS-FLANAGAN,
Ph.D. Professor of Counseling, University of Montana and author of *Clinical Interviewing and Suicide Assessment and Treatment Planning: A Strengths-Based Approach*

"It's hard to think of a more important topic than this. If you need a lifeline for a kid who got swept up in the hopelessness of 2020, pick up *Seen.*"

—JON ACUFF,
*New York Times* bestselling author of
*Soundtracks: The Surprising Solution to Overthinking*

"I cannot wait for *Seen* to get in the hands of parents, small group leaders, and anyone who works with the next generation. Thank you, Dr. Chinwé and Will for creating a mental health resource that is founded in both faith and psychology."

—SAM COLLIER,
bestselling author of *A Greater Story*,
and Lead Pastor of Hillsong Atlanta

*C*

"*Seen* is the intervention that we all need! This text clearly articulates the connection between the brain, body, and despair with references to research on trauma processing, neuroscience, attachment, and child development. It also provides much needed case examples and practical techniques that anyone can use with children and adolescents who are in despair. If you're a parent, mental health professional, educator, *or* simply part of a child's village, you should be reading *Seen* right now!"

—LAYLA J. BONNER, PH.D.,
Assistant Professor of Counseling, Belmont University,
Licensed Marriage and Family Therapist

"*Seen* is a book for all of us. From parents to pastors, this book challenges us with hope, courage and commitment. Will Hutcherson and Dr. Chinwé tell inspiring stories and give practical advice on how to best add value to this struggling generation. Don't miss this exciting and riveting book that will stir your soul to action."

—KEVIN MONAHAN,
Next Gen Professor, Liberty University Online, and
Executive Pastor of Journey Church, Lakeworth, Fla.

"These words from Chinwé and Will are going to be balm to your anxious heart. With the rising trend of anxiety and depression in kids these days, the practical steps they give to help kids heal, along with the clinical data they cover, is exactly what we need in these times."

—CARLOS WHITTAKER,
bestselling author of *Kill the Spider:
Getting Rid of What's Really Holding You Back*

"I am thrilled how Will and Chinwé have clarified what is happening with this generation and despair. After reading *Seen* you'll be enlightened and know there is a reason to have hope!"

—KEVIN W. NORWOOD,
DMin, MaPT, Student Pastor, Owasso First Assembly

"What a timely book executed brilliantly by Chinwé and Will. You can feel the passion they have to help our children cope, deal, and heal. We need this now more than ever. A tool box, a guide, a true gift."

—SHANOLA HAMPTON,
wife, mom, pastor's daughter, director, producer,
award-winning actor best known for her role
as Veronica on Showtime's *Shameless*

"With increasing numbers of kids saying they're anxious (and increasing reasons for them to be so), parents and leaders have to go beyond the easy answers and seek to understand what their kids are feeling. This book by my friends Will Hutcherson and Chinwé Williams offers real and practical steps for parents who just aren't sure what to do next. Will approaches this from a ministry leader's perspective. Chinwé brings her experience as a licensed counselor to the conversation. With solid research, authentic examples and deep empathy, they help us all see what's right in front of us."

—REGGIE JOINER,
Founder and CEO of Orange, speaker,
and author of multiple books, including
*Don't Miss It* and his latest, *It's Personal*

"The mental health crisis facing today's children and youth is undoubtedly one of the greatest concerns for anyone working to help young people reach their full potential. As parents, educators, and community leaders, we must listen deeply to those who can provide real insight and practical assistance to help a generation move forward. As a mother, I'm grateful for Will and Chinwé's insight, scientific research, clinical observation, and ability to guide each of us to know both when and how to act."

—KRISTEN IVY
President of Orange and Parent Cue,
architect of "It's Just a Phase," educator,
and author of more than 30 books

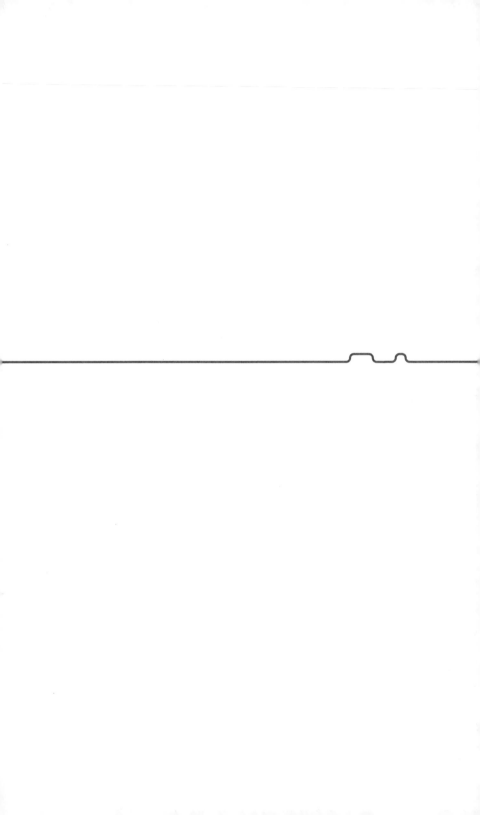

# SEEN

## HEALING DESPAIR AND ANXIETY IN KIDS AND TEENS THROUGH THE POWER OF CONNECTION

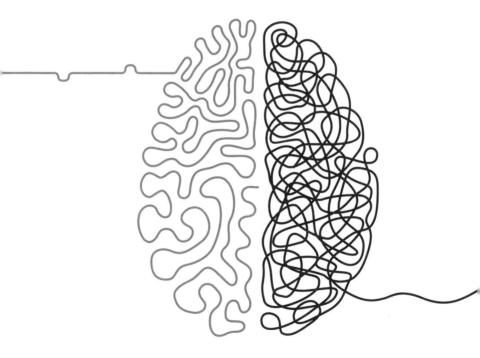

## BY WILL HUTCHERSON & CHINWÉ WILLIAMS, PH.D.

Seen: Healing Despair and Anxiety in Kids and Teens through the Power of Connection
Published by Parent Cue, a division of The reThink Group, Inc.
5870 Charlotte Lane, Suite 300
Cumming, GA 30040 U.S.A.

Other Parent Cue products are available online and direct from the publisher at
ParentCue.org. Bulk copies are available at store.thinkorange.com.

ISBN: 978-1-63570-104-3
©2021 Will Hutcherson & Chinwé Williams

Writing Team: Will Hutcherson & Chinwé Williams
Lead Editor: Karen Wilson
Creative Direction: Ashley Shugart & Meghan Hewitt
Cover Illustration: Getty Images
Book Interior Design & Layout: Jacob Hunt
Project Management: Brian Sharp
Director of Publishing: Mike Jeffries

Printed in the United States of America
First Edition 2021
4 5 6 7 8 9 10 11 12 13
06/08/2022

# TABLE OF CONTENTS

To the Hutch crew, Arianne—You are an example of deep connection and helping others feel seen, as I have received the benefits of your love and empathy.

To Liam, Reese, and Kinsley—Thanks for giving me grace and teaching me more than I've taught you.

To my family, friends, and mentors—Thank you.

**—WILL HUTCHERSON**

To the Williams tribe Lonnie, Bray, Noah, and Jailyn— I'm grateful for your love and endless support.

To Mom, Dad, and sibs—Simply thank you.
To Chima—I stand in awe of the gifts God has placed within you, thanks for sharing them.

To Tonya, Andrea, and Layla—Thank you for your faithful intercession. I'm forever grateful for your wisdom and encouragement. Because of all of you, I feel seen.

**—CHINWÉ WILLIAMS**

We both want to thank The Orange Team for making this book a reality. Karen Wilson, Mike Jeffries, Brian Sharp, and so many more—Thank you for your hard work and for loving kids, teens, small group leaders, churches, schools, and parents through projects like these.

Lastly, to those walking through "the dark night of the soul"— There is always hope.
Just keep breathing and keep connecting.

# PREFACE

## What We Need You to Know Before Reading This Book

In recent years, our world has seen a pandemic of depression, anxiety, and despair in kids and teenagers. In fact, the age group that has seen the highest increase in suicide rates is in kids age 10 to 14 years old.[1]

This book was written during a global health pandemic, which has presented even more challenges to the mental health of kids and teenagers. Adding to the crisis, centuries of racial injustice have come rushing to the center of our attention. Anger, fear, and hurt are boiling over in every community from the weight many feel over continued social injustice and racism.

The combination of social unrest, uncertainty, and isolation has resulted in traumatic reactions for many families. It will take years to fully know how the extraordinary circumstances in this new decade have impacted our society, especially its youngest members. Unfortunately, what we do know with certainty is that many people have experienced an increase in anxiety, distress, and a sense of helplessness, but likely it has increased even more so for kids and teens across the world.[2]

But this book isn't about the bad news.

This book is about *hope*.

**This book is about practical solutions for** parents, small group leaders, pastors, and caring adults to help heal despair in kids and teens.

## There Is Always Hope

Hope is the mantra our team has been sharing with teenagers in schools across the country. After working in youth ministry for over 15 years and encountering an increasing number of kids wrestling with depression and suicide, I (Will) set out on a mission to help fight this raging battle threatening a generation of youth.

Because of my studies in psychology, I had a hunch that healing despair starts in the brain. I suspected that the primary tools for healing likely included empathy and love and that human connection could help heal the brain in despair.

With the help of my friend Greg Hasek, a Licensed Mental Health Counselor, I started diving into the research. It turns out that I was onto something, and what we found was fascinating. People who are in despair experience a physical *dis-pairing* in the brain, which causes a person to become emotionally detached.

The good news I was looking for is that study after study from different disciplines of human sciences confirm that a relational connection can help the brain repair itself. Our brains are wired to heal, but it takes intentional steps in love and empathy—steps that I have found don't always come easy to us adults. Some of them are completely opposite of what we find in traditional parenting playbooks.

In 2018, I gathered a group of communicators, counselors, and educators to start a non-profit, Curate Hope. The goal was simple—to use our cumulative experience to partner with parents, churches, and schools to help heal despair in kids and teenagers.

Our team began traveling the country, encouraging hurting teens that there is always hope, even in the darkness of despair. While we helped many kids and teens flip the script to their story, we encountered many more parents, educators, and pastors who were looking for ways to help as well. Families and schools were looking to counselors and mental health professionals, only to find long waitlists or affordability challenges. I knew the best way to help kids was to empower those closest to them with the same healing tools we were learning to use. My journey to help leaders and parents walk with kids through dark times eventually led me to Dr. Chinwé Williams.

I (Chinwé) have been counseling children and teenagers and the adults who love them for close to twenty years. I started my counseling career as a high school counselor right out of graduate school. I was pretty young and relatively green when I began, and I felt frequently caught off-guard by the myriad of challenges many of my students faced. Depression, anxiety, low self-esteem, self-harming, and multiple forms of trauma—you name it, my students experienced it.

My students challenged me in the best possible way, and I remain grateful to God for those years, which have greatly informed my style and approach as a therapist today. What I've learned in my study of attachment theory and experienced in my clinical work with kids is that connection is key. I'll never forget what a mentor once told me, "Kids don't care what you know until they know that you care."

## Know This

If you picked up this book, maybe there is a person you deeply care about who is battling with depression, anxiety, or hopelessness. Perhaps you don't know what to do, or you're struggling to connect.

First, know that you are not alone. Parenting or leading a kid or teen struggling with despair is particularly difficult, and it can render one helpless. But remember, as Will mentioned in the very beginning, there is always hope, and there is plenty you can do right now without the benefit of a psychology degree.

Together, we will break down practical tools that will help the kids and teens you love battle despair. All of these tools are based on the latest in brain research and the science of attachment. Also, it's important to note that we wrote this book from a Christian viewpoint. Faith is an important part of our lives and we believe God helps us in our time of need. If you picked up this book but don't consider yourself a Christian or person of faith, we still believe you will be able to utilize the tools we will present.

So, with research in hand, we have set out to empower parents and caring adults. To give practical and easy to understand tools so parents don't feel helpless, stuck, or powerless against the invisible enemy of despair. To give you hope!

Before we go any further, let us first say this: There's no way a book this size can be an exhaustive dissertation on the mental health crisis in kids and teens. We hope this book will be a great **starting point** for parents and caring adults who want to understand what kids are facing and learn practical tools to help.

It's also important to understand that in this book, we have to make some generalizations. There are certain practices that can help contribute to mental health. However, this **does not mean** that if a child or teen is struggling with despair, depression, or thoughts of suicide, their parents and other caring adults in their lives aren't doing enough or didn't do enough. There are times when an individual that has been loved and cared for incredibly well struggles with depression or dies by suicide, and it simply doesn't make any sense.

If you're reading this, and you've lost a child to suicide, we are so incredibly sorry for your loss. We can't imagine the amount of pain you've endured and continue to endure every single day. We can only imagine the questions you've wrestled with—questions for which you may never have an answer. Please know that you also are not responsible for what happened. The human brain is very complex. And there are things we may never understand this side of heaven.

Our prayer is that these pages will not make you feel like you didn't do enough. Instead, we pray that the message we share will honor you and maybe even give you the smallest glimmer of hope. And though you've suffered indescribable loss, you too can be part of this change. You have something incredible to offer with your story. Something so precious and so deeply personal that though it may take all of the courage you can muster, opening your heart can help bring healing.

To every parent, small group leader, coach, pastor, and caring adult, please know that no matter how many times you feel you've messed up, you can *still* make a difference in the kids in your life. You don't have to execute these tools perfectly in order for them to work. Each intentional decision you make *matters*, including the decision to pick up this book.

This book *does* not and *could* not possibly address every situation or emotional health challenge that you will face as a caring adult. But we will provide you with helpful information that will enable you to better understand your kid and teen while recognizing just how important you are in his or her life.

**One last note**: Throughout this book we will tell stories from our experience counseling, guiding, and mentoring kids and teens. Names of individuals and identifying details or facts have been changed for confidentiality. Therefore, any identifying resemblance to actual individuals is merely coincidental.

Thank you for allowing us the privilege of adding to the conversation.

*Will Hutcherson and Chinwé Williams, Ph.D.*

# SEEN

# ONE
# OLD TOOLS

Tyler was one of my (Will's) favorite students. I know neither parents nor youth pastors are supposed to have favorites, but I loved spending time with Tyler. He was a great kid—funny, respectful, and smart.

As a seventeen-year-old, Tyler had a bright future. He was one of our top students in the leadership development program I was helping run at the time. He was committed and hard working. I would often see him pitching in to help others and was eager to offer a hand.

Though Tyler seemed to have it together on the outside, he was actually suffering from depression. He shared with me the struggle he had to get out of bed some mornings. Despite loving the program and the other students, Tyler had moments of self-doubt. In his worst moments, he even had thoughts of ending his life.

How does a kid who seemingly has it all together get so down? I mean, he has so much going for him, right?
He comes from a good family. *Check.*
He wasn't bullied as a kid. *Check.*

He didn't have any significant trauma from abuse. *Check.*

So, what was happening?

This scenario was becoming all-too-familiar. More and more teens like Tyler started popping up, and I knew there seemed to be more than a few instances of despair and depression. Students started coming into my office looking for guidance as they shared, "I think I have depression." Over and over again, I had parents or students approach me about the concerns they had for others.

"They just don't seem like themselves anymore."
"They're always down."
"She is saying some things that are really concerning me."

It seemed more and more students were feeling paralyzed and anxious when facing resistance or obstacles in life. Students were losing their resilience and their motivation. They seemed to have a pessimistic outlook about the future and were disengaging emotionally. I wanted to know more about what was causing this increasing disengagement or detachment in recent years, so I started asking questions and listening.

What I found didn't just concern me, but rather it *alarmed* me. Teenagers were facing high levels of despair. Some were self-diagnosing as being very depressed. Others were sharing about panic attacks or anxiety. At worst, they described their attempts to kill themselves or their future plan to kill themselves. Surprisingly it turns out, it isn't just my own community experiencing these trends. Despair has become a serious problem nationwide.

Here are some pretty startling statistics:

- Since 2007 . . .
  - ▶ Suicide rates have increased by 76 percent for ages 15 to 19.
  - ▶ Suicide rates have nearly doubled in teen girls.

- ▸ The highest rate of increase in suicide among all age groups is in kids between 10 and 14 years old.
- ▸ Depressive symptoms are up 21 percent in boys, and up 50 percent in girls.[3]

- ■ Suicide attempts among black teens increased by 73 percent between 1991 and 2017, and there is an elevated risk of suicide among African-American boys ages 5 to 11.[4]

- ■ In early 2020, an estimated 1 out of 4 young adults contemplated suicide.[5]

- ■ In March 2020, the *Disaster Distress Helpline* saw an increase of 891 percent in call volume.[6]

Many feel powerless against the depression and despair kids are facing today. All of us are scared, not wanting the story we've heard so many times to become the story of our own kids. So, we do our best with what we know.

## A Time When I Blew It

Remember my favorite student, Tyler? I saw so much potential in Tyler, and I wanted to help him reach it. I thought: *Maybe he just needs a push.* Perhaps Tyler just needed to be challenged and motivated to overcome his despair. If he could only see his true potential, then maybe his dark cloud would lift.

I'm embarrassed to confess these thoughts, but out of my goodwill, I devised a plan to "help" him. I worked with another program leader to map out a personal development plan focused on challenging Tyler and pushing him out of his comfort zone.

Over the following months, we executed our plan, fully expecting we'd have a completely new student in ninety days. Beaming with joy, he would then thank us for pushing him and helping him to see the positive side of life.

That's *not* what happened.

One weekend at a church retreat, Tyler had a major setback. Being away from family, in a spiritually charged environment he wasn't used to, his anxiety increased. He tried to share his feelings with another leader, but he was dismissed with trite responses like, "Well, man, just trust God and let's keep praying."

Later, on the second night, Tyler couldn't take it any longer. He felt so uncomfortable and alone that he called his parents, who drove two hours to pick him up. He left without telling anyone.

"He can't just leave without saying anything!" one leader blurted out as we all nodded our heads in agreement. With eyebrows lifted, another leader added, "Well, we are going to have a hard talk about this."

The following weeks after the retreat, the "hard talks" designed to help Tyler seemed to do the opposite. Our plan hadn't worked. Instead, Tyler became resistant to personal challenge, was disrespectful, and seemed angry. I didn't know what to do. Why couldn't he just change his attitude? I mean, "His attitude is his altitude!" Right? He just needed to snap out of his funk.

## Moment of Truth

The moment of truth came after a few months of working on our plan. Another retreat was coming up, but this time Tyler politely shared with another leader he wouldn't be going. I was furious and asked him to come to my office. But, when he tried to explain to me how he was feeling, I didn't listen. I was too busy thinking about the principle, rule, or statement I was going to say next.

"You know, you committed to going on this trip as part of our group. You need to see it through."

Tyler again tried to share his feelings with me.

"I understand you feel that way, but it doesn't matter. You need to get over how you're feeling and come with us."

Again, I wasn't listening. Frustrated and misunderstood, Tyler quit the program the next day.

**I blew it.**

I didn't realize it at the time, but I wasn't able to help Tyler because I was using "old tools." I was trying to fix him, offer simple solutions, toughen him up, and force change. These methods may have worked at one time and may even still work with some, but these tools are duds for most. This experience changed me, and I knew I had to learn a new approach.

It is easy to feel powerless, fearful, and not know what to do. Every parent, small group leader, and youth pastor is asking things like:

What can I do against this invisible enemy?
Am I missing something?
Am I doing the right things?
What are the right things?

## The Good News

Here is the good news:
*You are not powerless.*

The truth is you have a superpower. You really do. I'm not just over-hyping.

**Our greatest weapon against despair and suicide is *you*:**

Parents.
Small group leaders.
Youth pastors.
Caring adults.

It turns out, there are tools that can help kids and teenagers heal. Remember when we said our brains are wired for healing? They are! Our brains are designed to respond in predictable ways when we connect with others on a deep level and when we "feel seen." In fact, the research shows that we aren't powerless at all. For instance, research on the neuroscience of attachment shows us that the brain can learn a new attachment pattern because of the process of neuroplasticity. The brain has the ability to rewire and reorganize itself.

Another helpful discovery is that a secure attachment with an adult can not only help heal and rewire the brain from a past insecure attachment, but it can also help decrease the risk for despair and suicidal thoughts in adolescents.[7]

Whether you are a parent of a preschooler, elementary-aged kid, teenager, or young adult, you can begin habits now that will nurture emotionally healthy development and create resilience against despair when they are older.

If you know ANYONE who is facing any level of despair, there are practical things you can do right now to intervene and begin the process of healing. These are tools that will help you make significant connections that lead to change—tools I wish I had with Tyler.

I did many things wrong in my plan to help Tyler, but the greatest was my inability to see him and what he was feeling. He didn't feel *seen*. Ironically, if I had just connected and resisted the urge to "fix" him, I could have played a part in helping him to heal. Instead, I unknowingly played a part in keeping him right where he was.

I'm happy to report that Tyler is doing great today. He went to counseling and is managing his depression, and I learned a difficult lesson that shaped the journey I am on today. The true key to Tyler's success was his parents. They were deeply engaged. They prayed for him every day, and they instinctively used many of the tools we will share in this book.

These strategies are ground-tested and we believe they will empower you to be a part of the solution to the rising despair we are seeing in kids and teenagers. They will help you connect with, give hope to, and lead the next generation towards healing.

# TWO
# WHEN IN DESPAIR

Before we give you the tools that will help you lead a kid or teenager through despair, it's important to tell you a little more about the state of mind we're dealing with. And yes, it all starts in the brain.

I know, I know, you might be thinking, "I don't need a science lesson, just tell me how to help my kid." But it's important to know what's going on in a kid's head so you can understand why these tools work. It might just blow your mind.

The brain is made up of two parts. Actually, it's made up of a lot of parts. But we're going to break it down to the two hemispheres and two essential functions.

The *right* side of the brain is responsible for emotional processing. This is where the amygdala processes fear and other emotions that activate "fight, flight, or freeze" during stressful or dangerous situations. It's also the part of the brain affected by parent-child attachment (more on that later).

The *left* side of the brain is responsible for logical processing. This is the part of the brain where one's ability to plan and organize takes place. When we're calm, the left brain is able to be logical. But when we're upset, the right brain can take over and react from an emotional place. This is especially true of anyone who has an insecure parent-child attachment or previous traumatic experience.

In a healthy brain, processing goes back and forth between the two sides—emotional and logical. God designed our brains so we can feel lots of different emotions, but we're able to flip them over to cognitive processing. In other words, our emotions are *real*, but we have the ability to consider them logically and determine whether or not what we feel is actually *true*.

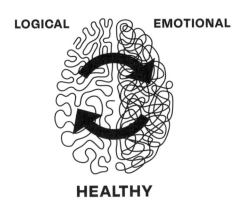

For example, if I hear a loud bang followed by the sound of shattering glass, I'm instinctively going to be startled. My heart rate will rise because my fight, flight, or freeze response has been triggered on the right side of my brain. But let's say I stop and look around. I am investigating (logical) and discover that a picture has fallen off the wall. Immediately, I take a deep breath, and my stress begins to subside.

Healthy functioning means we're able to deal with our emotions properly. The problem is when we can't logically process our emotions, something else takes place.

That something is **despair**.

## What Is Despair?

Despair is one of the hardest things a person can face. One theologian called despair "the dark night of the soul."[8]

The Bible, a text full of descriptions of authentic and raw emotions, references the word "despair" frequently. (We counted 28 instances.) The psalmist perhaps describes the feeling best, "Their insults have broken my heart, and I am in despair. If only one person would show some pity; if only one would turn and comfort me" (Psalms 69:20 NLT).

Despair is what someone feels when they become hopeless and disconnected from their emotional state. Psychologist Mark Goulston describes despair as a "dis-pairing, where two halves of the brain begin to separate.[9] This process is also called *emotional detachment*.

Here's what dis-pairing looks like in the brain:

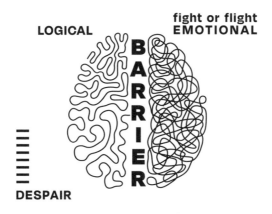

Experiencing stress causes cortisol—a stress hormone—to flood the brain. A constant drip of cortisol causes this detachment or dis-pairing. Understanding this matters because we need our logical processing to be able to navigate our emotions. When the two sides are detached, we can't navigate the constant flow of emotional signals.

This detachment explains why those in despair often feel numb. Some describe it like they're experiencing their life outside of themself because it's so difficult for them to identify how they really feel. They can become dissociated from their emotions. The risk of this detachment happening increases when something traumatic happens.

Trauma, as well as stresses of life, can cause the amygdala (the part of the brain where fight, flight, or freeze response is located) to become overactivated. This results in all of the emotions building up on the right side of the brain. All the blood flow starts to head that way. The brain essentially goes back to survival mode, and logical processing tends to break down.[10]

The challenge for adolescents is that their brains are still developing. The frontal cortex, which is responsible for higher-end thinking like judgment and decision-making, isn't fully developed. When you add despair, trauma, and stress to this already under-developed brain, it's no wonder how this dis-pairing takes place. Maybe you can relate. I'm sure you can. We have all faced levels of despair.

Have you ever gone through something extremely painful and had someone ask you how you feel? Perhaps you said something like, "I don't know how I feel" or, "I just feel numb." Sometimes kids and adults can get stuck in this place of numbness, where the right side of the brain is so overactivated that they're unable to put things into words or process their emotions.

## MEET CHLOE

I (Chinwé) met Chloe when she was 13 years old, approximately seven months after discovering her father lying on the kitchen floor—not breathing. Her small group leader had dropped her off at my office after experiencing yet another emotionally rough day. Chloe was struggling not just from the traumatic loss of her dad but also from the loss of memories she hoped they would share in the future. Chloe told me her story, tearfully vacillating between recurring thoughts of the coffee mug she had shattered on the floor next to her dad and their heated disagreement the previous night about a seventh-grade boy she had been texting.

Over the course of our time together, Chloe reported vivid and disturbing dreams that disrupted her quality of sleep. She also developed a noise sensitivity which resulted in escalating arguments with her busy twin sisters, who shared the adjoining room. Anxiety also began to set in.

Despair is often intertwined with anxiety. And anxiety can stem from trauma. Following a traumatic loss, stress-related hormones can initiate a heightened state of arousal in our nervous system. When we are chronically anxious, we become hyper-alert and continuously on the lookout for danger. This state of hyperarousal was difficult for Chloe to manage, leading her to miss several days of school each month.

"Am I crazy?" Chloe would periodically ask. I assured her that she was not—and attempted to explain that she was experiencing a physical reaction to an acutely stressful experience.

With her mother, grandparents, and small group rallying around her, Chloe eventually improved and became a "typical" high schooler. While she battled occasional waves of anxiety and despair, she functioned, overall, relatively well.

That is, until several years later, her boyfriend cheated on her and later broke up with her, setting her into a downward spiral. Then she began to self-harm.

Chloe and I reconnected through counseling, and I asked her directly about thoughts to end her life. She denied feeling suicidal, but when I asked her to share what she did feel, she said, "I feel nothing—just numb . . . emotionally dead inside."

Chloe's experience was not uncommon. I have counseled kids and many teenagers over the years who engaged in self-harming behaviors meant to release and cope with profound emotional pain—or *despair*.

I know, it's hard to think about a child intentionally hurting themselves. But for some kids, like Chloe, cutting seemed like the only way to disrupt the overwhelming pain of rejection and grief from two recent, painful losses.

Self-harming is viewed as an emotionally regulating behavior and the reasons why youth self-harm are complex. Many teens who self-harm do so as a way to distract from emotional pain, but also as a means to discover if they can "wake up" from an emotional slumber to feel *anything* following a long period of emotional numbness. Think of it this way, kids and teens who self-harm are desperately trying to bring the two sides of their brains back together. To feel something again. To feel anything.[11,12]

Chloe's story is an illustration of the contrasting nature of despair. For some youth battling despair, there can be excessive and overwhelming emotions, while others experience a profound sense of emptiness.

(*For more information on self-harm and how to respond to a kid or teen who is self-harming, see Appendix 1.)

## Emotionally Detached

At some point in our life, each of us has experienced the sensation of nothingness, feeling emotionally detached or numb following one event or a series of severely stressful events. Many of my clients commonly describe this experience as a "fog" or a temporary feeling of dissociation or disconnection from one's emotions, thoughts, or body. Several studies suggest that emotional numbness may be adaptive, meaning it developed as a way for our brain to help us cope with exposure to extreme or continual stress.

In an article written in the psychological journal, *Development Psychology,* the authors outlined the results of a six-year study that had followed nearly 3,500 children (between the ages of 3 and 12) who had been exposed to a violent incident. The study found that the children had become emotionally numb, regardless of age or gender.[13]

They also noted common factors that may lead to emotional numbness:

- Deeply emotional experiences such as the loss of a loved one

- Car crashes or near-death experiences

- Childhood emotional abuse, physical abuse, and/ or neglect

- Extreme interpersonal conflict or ongoing stress, usually with a family member or close friend

- Finding out about a terminal illness

Researchers also discovered that regardless of the reason for the dissociation, the good news is that, in most cases, the numbness eventually goes away with frequent engagement in self-care and support from others.

Parents and leaders, what you say and how you show up in your kid's or teen's life *really* matters. The way you respond to someone who is emotionally dead could actually lead them to feel more alive.

## The Power of Connection

Here's the incredible thing: Parents and caring adults have a supernatural ability to help kids heal from despair. This is possible because of the power of connection.

Research on attachment and neuroplasticity confirms that our **brains are wired to respond to love and empathy, even when we're in despair.** When we connect with another person, or when someone empathizes with us and helps us feel seen, the two sides of the brain begin to heal.

How does this happen? Oxytocin, a hormone responsible for healthy attachment, floods our brain and begins to bring the two sides back together. As we experience connection, love, empathy, and secure attachment, the two sides rejoin. As a result, despair lessens.

The brain's re-pairing can restore a wholeness that allows emotional processing to then flip over into logical processing. This happens in the context of healthy relationships. And it happens in the context of love.

No one modeled how to do this better than Jesus. He healed more than blind eyes and deaf ears; He healed hearts. Remember the woman He met at the well[14] and the one caught in adultery?[15] Jesus helped them to heal by showing love and empathy.

Parents, you have the ability to heal your kids through love and empathy faster and more effectively than any other person in your kid's life. Yes, small group leaders, teachers, grandparents, pastors, and other caring adults can help this process. But no one can do it better than you. You are the most influential voice in your child's life.

You are well-positioned because you have a connection that no one else does. **It's called Parent-Child Attachment.** In the early years of development, children form important and significant attachments to the caregivers in their life, most commonly their parents, that impact development over their lifespan. In fact, attachment styles, negative or positive, developed in the first two years go on to form an adult's framework of attachment with their future relationships—even their relationship with God.

The good news is that because of attachment, parents have a unique opportunity to connect with their child's emotions. They can distinguish and respond to their child's emotions like no one else.

Psychologists call this **attunement**.[16] We like to describe attunement as being in-sync or paired. It's when you feel understood, or rather, you feel *seen*. When someone can recognize what you're feeling and respond just how you need them to. Have you ever said, *"That person just gets me?"* If so, you're describing "feeling seen."

Some kids and teens facing despair do not feel seen. They feel alone. They think no one understands what they are going through. And most of the time, they think no one else feels the way they do. That doesn't mean you're not trying. Often, kids facing despair don't even know what they are feeling. It's challenging for them to put their emotions into words.

But everything changes when we tap into the power of connection, as a caring leader, friend, or parent, to help someone feel like they are truly seen.

Even though you are your kid's biggest ally and the best person who can help them, you aren't the only one they need. They need a team. You and they both need the help of teachers, coaches, pastors, and sometimes counselors and doctors. We realize outside support and professional help can be hard to find or even cost-prohibitive; that's why these tools are so necessary. But it's essential to do everything you can to take a wrap-around approach that envelops a kid with support and love.

The more parents, small group leaders, pastors, and caring adults use these pairing tools, the more kids will feel seen. The more connected kids feel, the more the two sides of the brain come back together. That's when healing takes place and where hope begins.

## Pairing Tools

So how do we help kids and teenagers feel seen? How do we help their brains move from being dis-paired to re-paired? How do we connect with our kids on a deep level to promote a secure attachment and influence healing when they are crippled with despair?

In the following pages, we will give you five practical tools you can use to bring hope into their darkened world. We call them *Pairing Tools*. These tools help create a healthy, secure attachment and a relational connection. They may seem simple at first glance, but research shows they have powerful effects on the brain.

> **Show Up**
> **See Them**
> **Just Listen**
> **Speak Life**
> **Build Grit**

If you are a parent with a kid or teenager who is in despair, fighting depression, or having suicidal thoughts, the good news is you *can* help them. These tools are for you. To give you hope when things seem hopeless and empower you to step more confidently toward connection and healing.

By no means are these a replacement to spiritual tools of prayer, the truth of God's word, or the power of faith. These tools are complementary to our faith. They are the practical actions. I am reminded of Mark Batterson's perspective on prayer, "Work like it depends on you. Pray like it depends on God."[17] After all, God often uses people to reach people.

Prayer is a powerful spiritual tool and the one we should always begin with. So, before we jump in, let's pause and ask God to go before us and begin the work in us, and in our kids and teenagers. Chinwé and I have already prayed so much for you and for the kids and teens you are connected with.

Will you pray this prayer with us now?

> God,
>
> I know you are the One who spoke my life into existence.
> I know you are with me, and you have not left me alone.
> You are the Great Healer.
> Today, I pray that you will go before us.
> Begin the healing work in our hearts and minds.
> Help me learn how to connect on a deeper level and use me as a tool in your hand to help others heal from despair.
>
> In Jesus' name, amen.

# THREE
# **SHOW UP**

The first pairing tool is foundational for helping a kid or teenager. So, if you don't read anything else, read this chapter. All the other pairing tools hinge on this one simple principle: **Show up**.

Why? Because presence influences healing more than anything.

I (Chinwé) received a phone call recently from one of my clients. Sharon, a mother, was concerned about her 15-year-old daughter Ella, who had started behaving differently. Sharon had noticed a sharp decline in Ella's mood; she was becoming irritable and spending more time alone. Ella was usually very social. She performed well in school, was active on the track team, and had a great group of friends. But something just seemed off. Sharon asked me for some advice. After speaking with them both, it seemed Ella was feeling disappointed about a boyfriend relationship. While she didn't seem to be thinking about harming herself, Sharon and I decided just to keep an eye on Ella and keep the conversation open.

A few days later, Sharon decided to check on Ella. She walked upstairs and sat down in Ella's room. Sharon knew she needed to take some time to be present with her daughter, but unaware yet how much her presence was actually needed. Using listening tools (we will share in another chapter), Ella slowly began to open up.

The defining moment came when Sharon asked a point-blank question.

"Ella, are you thinking about hurting yourself?"

Initially, Ella said, "I don't know."

Then, mom asked again more directly, "Are you having thoughts about taking your life?"

Ella paused, taking a deep breath before whispering, "Yes."

Sharon was petrified. Heartbroken and afraid, Sharon didn't know what to say but later reflected, "I just knew I couldn't leave her alone."

She replied, "I don't know what to do, but I love you. Is it okay if we call Dr. Chinwé to get help together?"

Ella obliged.

Sharon didn't want just to set up a therapist appointment. She knew she needed to help Ella in the moment and that she couldn't leave her alone. So, she sat with Ella, sometimes quietly and sometimes listening and offering support.

As the conversation unfolded, Ella admitted to frequently texting until the early morning and was not getting enough sleep. Sharon was shocked that Ella quickly gave up her phone upon request without a petition—another sign that Ella knew she needed help and was open to her mom's guidance. As the night came to an end, Ella said she was afraid to go to sleep.

"What can I do?" Mom asked. "Would you like to sleep in my room tonight?"

Ella shook her head, "No."

"Is it okay if I sleep in your bed with you?" Sharon asked (praying that her child would agree but knowing she couldn't force it.)

"No, Mom. But could you stay close by?" Ella asked.

She breathed a deep sigh of relief and ended up sleeping right outside her door.

## Outside-the-Door Presence

Can you imagine how Ella felt waking up the next morning, knowing she wasn't alone? Her mom was right outside the door. She showed up when she needed her most.

In moments of despair, the people we love need our "outside the door" kind of presence. That kind of presence creates safety like nothing else can. It may seem small, but when we *show up*, the brain responds in predictable ways.

Showing up is the first step to connection. It's like the Bluetooth button on your headphone or portable speaker. It starts the pairing process. Remember the parent-child attachment we discussed earlier? Showing up isn't the goal of parenting; secure attachment is the goal. But showing up is the beginning step to accomplish that goal. So how do you show up? Here are five ways:

## Show Up Before They Ask You To

If you are a parent of a teen, chances are since you're reading this, you already know that loving a teenager can require thick skin. There will be times they are embarrassed by you. There *will* be times when they push you away.

If we're not careful, over time, we can allow those moments to let us feel insecure. Eventually, we decide they don't need us anymore. Gone are the days when they would gleefully run into our arms when we walked in the door after a long day at work. But just because they aren't four years old anymore doesn't mean they don't still need us just as much as they did then—if not more.

Even though they are becoming more independent, you are still the parent. As the adult in the relationship, it's your responsibility to initiate quality time and conversation with them. Don't wait for them to ask you, because those times may get fewer and farther apart as they strive for independence.

## Show Up for What Matters to Them

Pay attention to what matters to them, and be willing to show up in their world—before they even ask you. This may mean you show up and do things with them that you maybe don't enjoy. During these times, it's important not to make this about you. It's about them.

- Go to their soccer games, dance recitals, or karate tournaments.

- Buy tickets to take them to see their favorite band in concert.

- Invite them to go to the opening night of that new superhero movie you know they're looking forward to.

- Take them to check out that video game they've been eyeing.

These are moments you show up with no agenda except to enjoy time with them, to cheer for them, and to give them a place to be themselves.

## Show Up When It's Inconvenient

There are moments when our kids face a crisis. These moments can be triggered by being bullied online, a pet passing away, a betrayal by a friend, a breakup, or losing a game. In moments like that, it's easier to know your presence is needed. But showing up doesn't only happen in crisis moments. It's in the small moments, too.

As parents, you've already been doing this their entire lives, calling into work to take care of a sick child or canceling date night to go to a kid's game. As they get older, it might look like picking them up from a party that got out of hand or staying up until 2 a.m. because they finally want to talk. I (Will) feel like my pre-teen becomes a deep theologian at bedtime and wants to ask me about life's greatest questions. As a pastor who works with kids and teenagers, I can tell you the most powerful, life-changing conversations happen late at night at camps and retreats when the adults would much rather be sleeping.

To show up means to be available, even when it's inconvenient.

## Show Up Often

To help our kids and teens in despair we have to show up often—every day. So, find ways to be *predictably available.*

I know a parent who started a nightly tradition to play a quick board game with her son before bed. He was facing despair after his family moved to a new city. Her son enjoyed getting to have a later bedtime than his siblings, and it was a moment he could count on every day. It wasn't the only thing this mom did, but it was a way to help communicate she was there predictably.

Here are a few ideas on how to show up often:

- Create a "conversation place" in your home. A place that is just for conversations. No phones, no screens, just people.

- Be intentional about creating moments. Be available during drive times, evenings, and bedtimes.

- If there is a time when you start to realize your kids are most likely to talk or open up, clear that time in your schedule.

- Text them occasionally to let them know you are thinking about them or praying for them. (Not to the extent you're stalking, of course.)

When it comes to kids in despair, showing up often in ways that aren't overbearing is essential to show them you care. But it also allows you to monitor their emotional state, so you know when something feels off.

## Show Up Undistracted

We often think of being over-connected to technology as being a problem for young people. But if we're really honest, we may find in our own lives a dependence on this distraction. Electronics and smartphones are amazing tools that aren't going away. I'm not arguing they should. However, when devices keep us as parents from being fully present, it can hinder our efforts to show up. We have to be intentional about showing up physically, mentally, and emotionally.

I (Will) am not a perfect parent. Let me tell you a story (in case you need a reason to believe me). As a parent of three young kids, I try to give them the attention that they need. But if I'm being honest, there are times when I "zone out." You know what I'm talking about.

Let me set the scene.

I'm at home, swiping through my phone, ignoring my kids. I mean, it wasn't my *goal* to ignore my kids, but I have "important" things to do. Who else will respond to Aunt Karen's politically-charged Facebook post, if not me? Who else will swipe through pages of Amazon and Wayfair home decor, if not me? And who else will binge watch that new Netflix series, if not me?

Kids waste time on electronics, but *never* me . . . I only do important things. Okay, okay, maybe I *do* waste time. This was one of those times.

One afternoon, I was looking at my phone, doing something important. My two-year-old daughter walked up to me and said, "Dad?"

No response.

"Dad?"

No response.

"DADDYYYYYY!"

Without looking up from my phone, I said, "Yes, Reese?"

But she wasn't satisfied with my response. She was so determined to get my attention, she grabbed my chin with her little hand, pulled my face towards her and said, "LOOK AT ME!"

It shocked me. Reese had never done that before, so I wasn't expecting it. Then and there, I had a choice to make: One, become frustrated and remind my two-year-old to have patience. Or two, allow my two-year-old to remind *me* to become *present*.

You see, she didn't just need me to acknowledge her. She needed to know she had my attention. To see her. She needed me to look her in the eyes and notice she was there. We like to give our kids a hard time about being on their screens, but we tend to be just as bad, don't we?

A 16-year-old girl recently said this to me, "I'm trying to talk to my parents about something, and they don't actually look at my face. They're just looking at the TV or their phones." She went on to share about how much that hurt. Her parents were unintentionally communicating that what they were doing on their phones was more important than what she had to say.

Phones and electronics aren't going away, and we hope they don't. Some of you might be reading this book on an electronic device. It's not about not using them; it's about boundaries.

We need them both for our kids and ourselves, so we can be fully present for those we care about.

## Show Up When They're Hurting

One of my favorite verses in the Bible is actually the shortest, "Jesus wept." This happens in John, Chapter 11 right before Jesus performs an incredible miracle by raising Lazarus from the dead. But before He does, He weeps. It's easy to pass by it quickly and skip to the miracle and miss the potency of what Jesus did. This is not my favorite verse for the fact that Jesus is sad, but it's **why** He is sad. In this moment Jesus is weeping because people He cared about were hurting. He hurt when they hurt. It is one of the greatest examples of empathy Jesus models for us.

Though Jesus knew He was about to perform a miracle and raise His friend Lazarus from the dead, He paused for a moment and just wept with Lazarus' family. Can you imagine how they felt? They felt that Jesus understood their sorrow. In that moment, they felt *seen*.

Jesus didn't just show up and blow it off with, "Mary, stop crying. It's going to be okay. Your brother is about to be alive again." Instead, He offered hope, and He paused to be with those who were hurting. John says, "When Jesus saw her weeping, and the Jews who had come along with her also weeping, he was deeply moved . . ." (John 11:33a, NIV).

Showing up is the beginning. It makes healing possible, because you're creating a secure attachment. When you create a secure attachment, kids and teens feel loved. Now, we can take even more steps to pair the brain's emotional and logical processing back together. The tools that follow will help you to maximize what happens when you show up so that you can create a deep connection—one that brings healing.

Don't be intimidated. The goal isn't to be a perfect parent or mentor or caring adult. Just be intentional and know this: Simply showing up is fifty percent of the work. Sharon didn't know all the right things to say to Ella. But she knew how to show up when she was hurting. She was present enough in her life already to know that something was not right, and knew when she needed to draw closer. That was the starting point that helped Ella begin to heal.

When you show up, the pairing process begins. Now that you're face to face, you can begin to really *see them*.

# APPLICATION EXERCISES
How Can I Apply This Tool?

1. Part of showing up means slowing down. Take a few moments to think about how you can create space in your everyday schedule for conversations with the kid or teen you are parenting or mentoring. Life is busy for us as adults and it may feel impossible to be there for busy teens every day (we barely see them as it is!). Our friends at ParentCue.org have identified four key times parents and teenagers may have together on a consistent basis:

**MORNING TIME:** Instill purpose by starting off their day with encouraging words.

**MEAL TIME:** Connect regularly by scheduling time to eat together.

**BED TIME:** Interpret life when they occasionally open up at the end of the day.

**THEIR TIME:** Strengthen your relationship by adjusting your plans to show up when they need you.

2. If you're a coach, consider setting time aside for ten minutes before practice starts to check-in. Or parents, consider creating a regularly scheduled game night or backyard bonfire night to spark conversation.Create a conversation space in your house. Designate a specific room or a set of chairs as a "no phone and no judgment" zone. For instance, make the family dinner table a device free table.

3. Show up especially when they are hurting or they've had a tough day. Here are a few ways to show up in a practical way:

   - Text them a screenshot of an encouraging quote.
   - Put their favorite snack in their room with a note.
   - Pick them up early from school and do something fun together.

   Take them on a short two or three-day trip camping, fishing, or watching their favorite sports team.

# FOUR
# SEE THEM

Have you ever asked your kids to do something you felt was simple, like, "Hey, can you take out the trash?" But they react as if you had asked them to climb Mount Everest with their bare hands.

One day, I (Will) asked my nine-year-old son Liam to clean his room. He had just finished school, and I was working in my home office. Liam protested, "But Dad, I was hoping we could play Legos® together."

"Buddy, I'm sorry. I can't do that right now. I told you earlier you would need to clean your room today, so it's time to clean your room."

"But, Dad . . ." Liam began to dig in. I could see we were starting a power tug-of-war.

I decided to try to break the cycle by incentivizing my ask.

"I'll give you three dollars if you clean your room, but if you don't, you'll owe me three dollars from your piggy bank." I knew he was saving up for something he wanted, so I felt like this was a safe bet.

A few minutes later, Liam called my bluff and came into my office with three dollars. I explained I didn't want his money; I was trying to encourage him to clean his room, and I still wanted him to clean his room. He began to complain and protest. "Can you *help* me clean my room?" "No, son, I have work to do."

"But, Dad . . ." I can't do it alone!"

My tone changed even more as I lost my cool, "Liam, I'm done talking about this. Go clean your room!"

He stormed off.

A few minutes later, Liam returned, this time with *all* of his money from his piggy bank. Tearfully, he threw it towards me and shouted, "Take all my money! Take it all. If that is what it takes to spend time with you!"

It was in that moment, with dollar bills and a thousand pennies scattered on my lap, that I saw things clearly. I could *see* him. I looked deeper than disobedient behavior. I could *see* a little boy desperately trying to communicate a need for connection.

I immediately stopped what I was doing, turned away from my computer, and got down on one knee. Looking him in the eyes, I said, "I'm sorry." I can see you are hurt and that you were trying to tell me you wanted to spend time with me."

For whatever reason, Liam was feeling disconnected and needed time to reconnect and feel safe again. He just didn't know how to express what he needed. Unfortunately, I was slow to acknowledge it.

Helping kids with emotional processing is uncomfortable for many, especially men, who tend to avoid dealing with their emotions. I get it. Raising my kids and using these tools has been the hardest thing I've ever done in my life. You see, I didn't grow up with a dad. I hadn't even seen a picture of my dad until I met him when I was 25 years old. I have no context of what a dad looks like—not even a bad one.

Naturally, I am not an emotional person. My hard-wiring is set for a ton of logical processing, and I prefer to believe that emotions, especially my own, are not valid unless they are logical.

In some ways, that's not all bad, after all, not all feelings should be acted upon. All feelings *should* be *acknowledged*. Growth happens when we learn how to recognize feelings and discern how to act on them appropriately.

However, I've learned my kids don't care if their feelings are logical. All they know is . . .

> I'm hurt,
> I'm sad,
> I'm disappointed,
> I'm angry.

AND the only question they have at that moment is, **"Do you *see* me?"**

We need to remember that when we show up, slowing down enough to see them and acknowledge their emotions in the moment, we can *eventually* lead them to process those emotions to help them logically make wise choices. But we start by first paying attention to their feelings.

For some, like me, acknowledging feelings can be uncomfortable. But I promise it's worth the discomfort. It may seem like you are softening and losing a part of yourself. Or maybe you fear your kids won't have the resilience or grit to overcome obstacles if you do. You want your kids to be tough because it's a tough world.

It *is* a tough world AND it's an *emotional* world, too. The best way to help kids and teens have the grit and resilience to overcome, especially when facing painful emotions, is to teach them to acknowledge their feelings and process them in healthy ways.

To lead kids and teenagers, first you have to *see* them. When they feel seen, you win their heart. Seeing them requires us to look beyond how they behave on the outside to try and understand what they may be feeling on the inside.

## See Beyond the Behavior

When a kid is facing a degree of despair, their behaviors may not be ideal. Irritability, moodiness, pulling away, or shutting down are behaviors you may experience. To see beyond the behavior, we must know the context. As a youth leader, when I feel frustrated at how a kid or student is behaving, I often remind myself that there is always more to the story. There is always more beyond the eye rolls, the snarky comments, or the anger.

I have to ask myself the question, "Do I know where they are coming from?"

For instance . . .

- What may have happened earlier that day?

- What trust has been eroded from past disappointments?

- What kind of trauma have they experienced from the pain of poverty or a high crime neighborhood?

- What social pressures might they be facing that we have no idea about?

- What kind of pain are they carrying from the daily reminders of political and social injustice?

- What shame might they be carrying from poor decisions or an abusive situation?

Parents, you might have a better idea of knowing where your kids are coming from. You know where they live, and you have tracked so much of their journey, but you probably don't know everything they are facing. And for those of us who are caring adults, coaches, small group leaders, or youth pastors, we often don't know unless we ask.

All these questions bring context. Context often creates empathy. Empathy to see beyond. Instead of asking, "Why are they acting this way?" we ask, "Do I know where they are coming from?

## See What They Feel

If you want to get in tune with your kids, you have to see past their behavior and understand what they are really feeling. The best place to start is to avoid shaming, labeling, or dismissing.[18] Let us give you an example. Your teenage daughter comes home and is distraught because she failed her math test. She throws her backpack on the ground and starts to cry.

There are a few ways you might respond logically. Your knee-jerk response might be to respond in ways that shame, label, or dismiss. For instance:

> **Shaming:** "What do you mean you failed your test?! Well, that was stupid. What were you thinking?"

> **Labeling:** "You failed your test because you're being lazy. You need to work harder, play fewer video games, and you'll get rewarded. God helps those who help themselves."

> **Dismissing:** "It's okay. There is no need to be upset. It's just one grade."

Although your response may be logical, here's what you might not realize. When you jump straight to logic without first acknowledging their feelings, you invalidate their emotions. Dismissing their emotions can worsen feelings of loneliness or beliefs that no one "gets them." This is especially true when a kid or teen is experiencing despair. As we said before, you have to *first* acknowledge their emotions before trying to use logic.

**Instead of shaming, empathize:**
"I know it's disappointing to fail a test. I get it. I hate it when I fail, too."

**Instead of labeling, look deeper:**
"I can see you care about your grades and especially this test. Tell me more about what's going on."

**Instead of dismissing, acknowledge:**
"I am so sorry you failed your test. You must feel disappointed. Tell me more."

**To help kids in despair, you _have_ to meet emotion with emotion and logic with logic.**

In other words, _meet right brain with right brain and left brain with left brain._ If a kid comes to you with emotion, that's where you meet them. If you don't, you're going to miss them completely.

If you feel the feeling _with them,_ then you'll have the opportunity to lead them to a place of logical processing. And as you make efforts to see beyond the behavior, they feel _seen._ As they learn how to move from emotional processing to logical processing, feelings of despair will diminish.

Think about it this way . . . It's like an emotional exhale. Sometimes kids and teens can feel so incredibly overwhelmed it feels like the only option is to keep it all in. Stuff it down. Not tell anyone. There's no outlet to talk about feelings or acknowledge emotions.

Imagine taking a BIG breath of air and not being able to exhale. What would happen? Your face turns red, your body tenses up, and you begin to shake. But then there comes a moment when you can't keep it all in anymore, and you EXHALE.

**Emotional processing is like an emotional exhale.** Talking to someone about your feelings is how you _emotionally exhale._ Simply expressing out loud what's going on in your heart helps to relieve the pressure. It lets out all that energy built up on the right side of the brain and in the body, allowing it to process out, shifting the energy to the left, where logical processing can occur.

It's not uncommon for those in despair to have difficulty expressing the emotions they are feeling. Often, when I (Will) ask a teenager who is experiencing despair how they feel, their response is "I don't know" or, "I feel numb." If that happens, try using these seven words to continue (not force) the conversation by asking:

**Do you feel . . .**

- Lonely?
- Hurt?
- Angry?
- Embarrassed?
- Ashamed?
- Alone?
- Afraid?

They may say, "I feel all of them!" If so, simply ask them to pick one and tell you more about it.

Another option is pulling up a picture of a *Feelings Wheel* (like the one ParentCue.org has adapted on the next page) and asking a kid or teen to pick one emotion they are feeling and tell you more about it. The *Feelings Wheel* is an excellent tool for helping identify the emotions a kid or teen may not have even realized they had. When we help them exhale their emotions, they begin to feel seen, which leads to a stronger connection and toward healing.

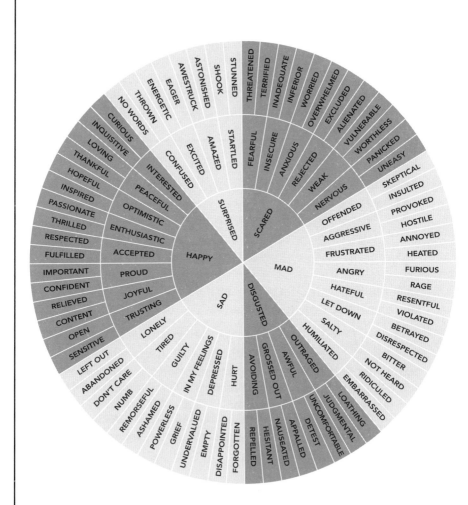

**FEELINGS WHEEL**

## See Beyond Despair: When It's Something More

When we begin to see things in the context of what is happening in a kid's life, and pay attention to their emotions, it becomes easier to recognize when despair might be moving into something more complex.

### MEET MARCUS

Marcus was an adventurous, sensitive, and fun-loving eleven-year-old with a great sense of humor. He was carefree and happy. The summer before I (Chinwé) met Marcus, his mother Rachel suffered a stroke that affected her speech and the majority of the right side of her body.

Initially, Marcus appeared to cope with the news as well as anyone would expect. But beneath the surface, there was a deep aching. In our first meeting, he shared that he recently told a neighbor he wanted to run away and never come back, believing that if he hid in the basement, nobody would notice his absence—for at least a few days.

Marcus was raised to believe in a loving God, but since his mother's stroke, he'd lie in bed for hours contemplating his beliefs and life's purpose. He began to lose focus at school, and his grades began to slip. He was an excellent lacrosse player but suddenly began to miss practices, and eventually, games—opting to distract himself with numbing video games instead. He would often play his favorite video game well into the night. His parents grew more concerned as Marcus grew more despondent.

One evening following another missed game, Marcus's dad and the assistant lacrosse coach visited Marcus in his bedroom. And, they kept visiting. They decided to keep showing up, doing very little talking, other than asking about *Fortnite*. Lacrosse never came back up; they just chose to show up to let Marcus know he was loved.

Gradually, Marcus's despair lifted, and he regained his faith in God and hope for the future. Even in loving and supportive families, the news of a life-threatening illness can shatter a kid's world and trigger overwhelming distress.

Marcus, unable to process intense and confusing emotions, is an example of someone who suffered from a temporary form of despair that therapists identify as *situational despair* or *situational depression*.

## Despair vs. Depression: What's the Difference?

You may be wondering what distinguishes *despair* from something more complex-sounding like *situational depression* or *clinical depression.* These are all terms used interchangeably in conversations, but have some very important distinctions.

Depression is often used as an umbrella term that covers a range of emotions from a passing sense of discouragement and feeling "blue" to a profound sense of hopelessness. As adults, each of us can attest to experiencing good days and bad days associated with the ups and downs and frustrations of human existence: a strained relationship, thwarted, long-anticipated plans, or a toxic work environment.

Keep in mind that depending on the event, those feelings of sadness or loss can last a few minutes, a few hours, a few days, or even weeks. Feelings of loss or sadness make sense—given any of those scenarios for adults or for young people.

Unhappiness is a part of life. Jesus Himself reminds us of that very fact when He says, "In this world, you will have trouble" (John 16:33, NIV).

However, in recent years we have noticed that our society has gone a bit far in characterizing any sense of unease as anxiety and any sense of unhappiness as depression. That can be problematic.

Similar to the word "trauma," the term "depression" has been overused and widely applied in popular culture, which can dilute the seriousness of actual depression. As parents and caring adults, we need to remain vigilant to recognize symptoms of depression, but we should also be cautious **not** to label kids with a diagnosis. In other words, we never want to minimize the severity of depressive-like symptoms, but we also don't want to shift into panic mode.

Child and adolescent mood disorders are often complex, not neatly categorized, and therefore, not very well understood. For example, feeling sad is a part of both despair and depression, and also normal life. However, it is important to develop some level of understanding about the differences between *despair, situational depression,* and *clinical depression* in order to know when it is time to seek professional support for your teenager. In what follows, we will unravel the distinctions between the three terms.

Let's begin with despair.

## Despair

Despair, like depression, can be temporarily debilitating. Despair is a profound feeling of discouragement and negativism about most things, particularly the future.

My clients in despair often express feelings of . . .
pain,
anguish,
loss of hope,
and loss of joy.

However, despair differs from episodes of clinical depression in that your kid or teen can typically (but not always) complete daily tasks. For example, they may be able to attend school, athletic events, or small group meetings and function somewhat normally despite their overwhelming feelings of heaviness.

## Situational Depression

Situational depression is a temporary condition that occurs when an individual has difficulty coping with or adjusting to a major life change, crisis, or event. In the case of Marcus and his mom's sudden stroke, life became very different—very fast. Situational depression is essentially a condition that develops as a reaction to an extremely stressful event.

Although situational depression can sometimes feel almost as heavy and dismal as clinical depression, it doesn't typically involve as many of the more severe symptoms that are often associated with clinical depression such as suicidal thoughts.

## Clinical Depression

If your kid or teen is clinically depressed, what they are experiencing goes well beyond adolescent "moodiness."

Clinical depression, also known as major depression, is a severe form of depression marked by persistent sadness, feelings of inadequacy, and a greatly diminished quality of life, among other things.[19] If your teen is clinically depressed, he or she may express difficulty concentrating, which makes simple decisions feel like monumental tasks.

According to prevalence rates issued by the National Institute of Mental Health, an estimated 3.2 million teens aged 12 to 17 in the United States had at least one major clinical depressive episode. The prevalence rate was higher among teen females (20%) compared to teen males (6.8%) and was highest among multi-racial teens.[20]

In youth, other symptoms of clinical depression include:

- Continued sadness and hopelessness
- Feelings of guilt or worthlessness
- Pervasive worry and anxiety
- Loss of interest in once enjoyable activities
- Lack of energy and fatigue
- Withdrawal from friends or loved ones or isolation

- Lack of concentration, difficulty with memory, or difficulty making decisions
- Sleeping too little or sleeping too much
- Unexplained aches and pains
- Thoughts of self-harm
- Preoccupation with death or thoughts of dying

Different from despair, a kid or teen struggling with clinical depression experiences most of these symptoms most of the day, nearly every day, and it impacts their overall functioning. It is worth mentioning that in order to be diagnosed with clinical depression by a mental health professional, an individual would have to exhibit several of these symptoms for at least two weeks.

## What Causes Despair or Depression?

When attempting to help someone who is hurting, one question that naturally surfaces is, "What happened to cause this?"

I probably get asked this question the most when having conversations about youth depression and despair.

Here's the thing. Behavioral health researchers still don't have a clear idea about how much of clinical depression is due to pure biology (genetic or biochemical factors) or psychology (learned behavior or life events).

One aspect of clinical depression that usually helps to distinguish it from situational depression or despair relates to trigger points. There isn't necessarily a trigger or an obvious event that acts as the catalyst for symptoms to surface. Many of the young people that I've counseled over the years frequently report vague feelings of guilt that really have no root and would seem "silly" to an untrained listener.

Consequently, the disheartening part for many parents or mentors is that your child or teen, like Tyler from chapter one, may have a life that is enviable to most—a strong support system, a loving family, numerous friends, academic success, a wonderful sense of humor—and still experience clinical depression.

If you suspect your kid or teen is experiencing depression, seek help from a pediatrician, primary care doctor, or therapist.

## See the Red Flags!

Suicidal Thoughts:

Finally, in *any* form of depression (or despair), the pain can become so deep that thoughts of taking one's life will begin to seize the mind. Whether experiencing situational despair or clinical depression, suicidal ideation has become a major problem for kids and teenagers.

Let's take a moment to debunk a myth:
Depression alone **does not** lead to suicide.
Despair **is** the main cause of suicide.

Let us explain.

Yes, many of the individuals who attempted or completed suicide had been diagnosed with clinical depression.[21] Depression can certainly contribute to suicide, along with other mental health issues, but depression alone does not *cause* suicide. The one common factor that everyone who faces suicidal thoughts feels is **despair or a sense of hopelessness**. This is important because we don't want to be quick to label when someone is facing suicide ideation. The bottom line is simply, when a kid or teenager is facing suicidal thoughts, do not navigate it alone.

## Why Does This Matter?

Even if a child or teen does not have a history or is not presenting depressive symptoms **BUT has communicated suicidal thoughts, it should always be taken seriously.** This means we have to attend to kids who are generally happy when they go through a difficult time. For example, don't immediately dismiss a heartbroken 15-year-old girl who says she doesn't want to live anymore as "attention-seeking."

Just because a child is not clinically depressed does not mean they aren't facing despair or suicidal thoughts. If a kid in your life says something concerning, express empathy, inquire about feelings of hopelessness and social disconnection, and validate their feelings.[22] Finally, ASK directly: *Are you having thoughts of dying or ending your life?* Or, *Are you thinking about hurting yourself?* The reason why you want to ask a direct question is to look for a *plan* or *intent*. Just because a kid says, "I don't want to be here," doesn't necessarily mean they have a plan to hurt themselves, but it *does* mean it's important to take action and do something about it.

Not every kid or teen who says they want to die will act on It. In fact, suicidal plans may or may not be associated with suicidal intent. Thoughts of suicide tend to increase when kids and teens feel socially disconnected, alienated, or rejected.

According to researchers, what pushes individuals to act on suicide as a way to alleviate distress is a dangerous combination of heightened psychological pain and limited problem-coping skills merged with arousal or agitation.[23]

One of the main reasons we wrote this book was for parents with kids or teens experiencing suicidal ideation. Often, parents feel powerless about getting outside help. Finding professional help is important in this situation, but now that we understand attachment, we know parents can play a crucial part in promoting healing and repairing the brain.

(*For more on what to do if your kid is having suicidal thoughts, turn to Appendix 2.)

For immediate help, contact the National Suicide Prevention Hotline by calling 1-800-273-8255 (TALK) or visiting SuicidePreventionLifeline.org.

These are professionals, trained to help you and your child de-escalate from a crisis moment to a place of safety and sustainability.

# APPLICATION EXERCISES
## How Can I Apply This Tool?

1. When you see an emotional reaction from a kid or teenager, try to respond first with empathy. Use the phrase, "I can see that you feel . . ." Practice making your first response a right brain response to encourage an emotional exhale. Ask questions about how they are feeling. If possible, pull up a feelings chart or wheel. If that's not readily available, have a few feeling words available as examples.

    **Do you feel . . .**

    - Lonely?
    - Hurt?
    - Angry?
    - Embarrassed?
    - Ashamed?
    - Alone?
    - Afraid?

2. We know that kids and teenagers can experience a roller coaster of emotions—calm one minute and hysterical the next—and still be normal. However, when you observe signs that appear to extend beyond teenage moodiness or kid brooding, it's important to intervene. Here are some ways:

    - Be aware of the classic signs of depression such as sadness, tearfulness, feelings of worthlessness or guilt, difficulty concentrating, changes in sleep and/ or appetite, and loss of interest in friends or typically enjoyable activities. If these signs persist on a daily basis, consider scheduling an evaluation with a pediatrician or therapist.

    - Check in. Talk to your kid or teen about the changes in mood or behaviors you've observed. In the conversation, try to determine if what they are experiencing is something that they believe they can eventually tackle or if life feels overwhelming right now. Encourage the expression of all emotions, even the really strong and complicated ones. Keep in mind that if emotions aren't freely expressed, they get bottled up and eventually leak out in unexpected ways.

- Seek professional support. If you think your kid or teen may be severely depressed, or if you have concerns about his or her safety, it's important to seek out professional support. Unfortunately, clinical depression isn't likely to improve on its own. Don't know where to begin? Start with a medical health provider like a pediatrician, family doctor, or school nurse.

3. If a kid in your life says something that concerns you, here are things that you can do in the moment:

- Express empathy for their distress, "It sounds like things are really hard for you right now. It doesn't seem like you have much hope that things will get better. Is that right?"

- Then ASK directly: **Are you thinking about hurting yourself?** Avoid using the word "suicide." That word may not connect with a kid or teen who is thinking about hurting themself. They may not be that far in their thoughts or understand the weight of those terms.

- Be sure to share your concerns with a healthcare provider. If you are a ministry leader or coach, tell the kid or teen's parents immediately.

# FIVE
# JUST LISTEN

You may have heard the phrase, "Hurting people hurt people." It means when we are in distress, our responses, words, and actions may hurt others around us. This makes sense when you look at how the brain is wired.

When a kid or teen is in despair, the amygdala (the part of the brain that controls fight, flight, or freeze) is activated. It's like a loud alarm constantly going off in their brains, telling them they are not safe.

It can be so hard to think.

This creates two huge challenges, one for the person in despair and the other for the person trying to be there for them. For someone in despair, trying to formulate words and express the emotion they are feeling can be really, really hard. It takes time and a feeling of safety to open up.

For the kid or teen managing anxiety or despair, the words and the emotions they express may not always feel kind or considerate. However, it's important to accept BIG emotions—theirs and yours.

For the person trying to help, the challenge is to not be triggered into a stress response while the person in despair is talking. This is especially true for parents. Our kids have the ability to cause us to "freak out" faster than anyone.

Often, hurting kids may even direct blame for why they are feeling the way they are towards their parents. This can be very difficult. It triggers insecurity and guilt about not being a good-enough parent. Our own shame cycle can kick in very quickly, putting us on the defense. A defensive posture is the greatest risk to a breakdown in helping our kids process their emotions.

Despite these two challenges, listening is a key pairing tool to reduce feelings of despair and promote healing.[24] As we mentioned in the last chapter, the ability to exhale emotions, moving energy and thoughts from the right side of the brain to the left side, helps shut off the amygdala alarm.[25] The key for parents, leaders, and caretakers is knowing how to actively listen while this is happening.

## Be a Safe Person

When you listen well, you communicate safety. That can happen with both words and body language.

### MEET JEN AND MELISSA

A few years back, I (Will) was working with a mother and teenage daughter. The mom, Jen, called me concerned about her daughter Melissa. She was showing signs of despair. Melissa had dropped out of school recently to take care of her new baby boy. Dynamics between her and the baby's father were starting to unravel. He was beginning to become aggressive and controlling. She was scared, was spiraling emotionally, and had no idea how to get out of a bad situation.

Both mom and daughter met with me to share what was going on. Jen was desperate for help and some direction. Melissa came reluctantly, afraid of what a "meeting with someone to help" would really mean. Another lecture? More shame?

As the two of them talked, I listened. Soon I started to see a pattern. Jen was talking 80 percent of the time, while Melissa was mostly quiet. After a while, I explained how the stress response works in the brain and the importance of feeling safe. To help them both see the benefits of this, I decided to try a little exercise. I had them face each other, and I asked the mom to hold her daughter's hands. I challenged them both to two minutes of locking eyes and not looking away. Then, I asked mom to affirm her daughter with loving and safety-filled words.

I'll admit, the first minute was weird. The two ladies sat across a coffee-shop table holding hands and locking eyes as Jen calmly shared affirming words. Melissa's shoulders were tensed in a shrugged position, her face tight with a look of discomfort and embarrassment. But after the first 60 seconds, something began to happen. The daughter's shoulders started to lower. Her face started to soften. Her eyes locked on her mother's eyes with a look that said, "Keep going." Two minutes later, the scene was drastically different from where it started. Melissa was unguarded and calm. When I asked her how she felt, she replied, "I feel relaxed."

She felt safe.

From there, the environment shifted. She started opening up as Jen listened. I helped guide the conversation from time to time with a few questions to encourage conversation, but I was mostly a spectator to a mom and daughter connecting on a deeper level. When you practice the art of listening well, you create a sense of safety. But knowing how to listen doesn't come naturally, especially if you're a "fixer" or have lots of things to say yourself.

Now, how do you focus on just listening? Well first, you direct all your focus on the other person. You get them talking. You let them get their feelings out. You let them emotionally exhale.

All of this happens when we start listening. But then, how do you convince them that you are actually hearing what they are saying so that they keep talking? How do you keep the pathways open so they feel safe and keep sharing the deeper parts of their soul?

## Talk Less

Good listening starts by making sure you're not the one doing most of the talking. James tells us in the Bible, "You must all be quick to listen, slow to speak, and slow to get angry" (James 1:10 NLT). We need to take this to heart when listening to our kids and teenagers.

It should make it easier when we can forget about teaching or saying the "right thing." Too often, instead of truly listening, we are thinking about what we're going to say next. Instead, focus on what the other person has to say. Your presence is more important than your words.

Yes, we all feel we have a lot of wisdom to share and a lot of life experience under our belt, but this is not the time to share it. Avoid lecturing at all costs if you don't want to automatically activate the "shutdown switch." More helpful and mutually-engaging teaching moments can come later, but not right now. Teaching activates the left side of the brain, the logical processing. And remember, we're aiming to help them *emotionally process*—which happens on the right side. So, when trying to help someone decrease feelings of despair, it's all about listening and then listening **some more**.

One of the most powerful responses you can give when a teen or kid starts talking and telling you how they feel is simply saying, "Tell me more." A "tell me more" posture gives the other person the platform, shows them you are interested in what they are saying, and it gives them a safe place to continue to emotionally exhale.

## Watch Your Tone

**What we say matters, but *how* we say it matters even more.**

Let's be honest, responding to someone who is in despair can be stressful, and if it persists, exhausting. Sometimes when we say something, it may not come out in the right way. For instance, there's a big difference between saying "I understand" with a soft tone and lifted eye-brows, and saying "I understand" in a monotone voice with a scowl. Tone matters, because it affects how kids interpret what we say.

You have the opportunity to set the tone in the conversation by responding calmly and lovingly. Remember, it's important in these moments not to emotionally react, freak out, or get defensive in any way, so leave your insecurities at the door. You can set the tone with your body language, too, so try not to make faces or react physically. If you falter—and we all do—refocus, apologize if you need to, and begin again.

Your calm responses and your warm tone will keep the conversation going, but eye-contact and appropriate physical touch can have profound effects on kids in despair, too. Why? Because nothing is more powerful than empathy and love. Connecting with your eyes and through appropriate touch helps a kid feel safe and communicates you are listening in a very practical way.

## Make Eye Contact

As we mentioned earlier in this book, the brain reroutes back to places of safety and early nurturement in times of distress. Eye contact, even from birth, is a part of what creates a healthy, secure attachment.[26,27]

The first two years of a child's life are rich and full of unique opportunities for secure attachment. Infants and toddlers learn and develop rapidly in an environment where they receive affection, attention, and encouragement.[28] These are the years before a child even speaks. It's in these first few precious years that a child learns whether they are lovable and safe, and if they can trust people to be there for them to fulfill their needs. Infants and toddlers learn and develop rapidly when they receive affection, attention, and nourishment. For instance, one of the most important ways a mother can connect to a baby and nurture a secure attachment is by looking in their eyes and holding them closely while feeding them.

Looking into a child's eyes even as they get older is an important way to reconnect, and it can help rewire their brains toward a healthy attachment. For most kids and teens, this works to promote safety and reduce anxiety, especially when in a heightened place of stress and despair.

When we pause and look at our kids *in the eyes* for an extended period of time, and we speak loving and affirming words, something takes place in the brain.[29] It takes them back to a place of safety and nurture, and it lowers feelings of despair. Because they feel *seen*. They feel like somebody understands them and is listening to them in a very real way. (We discuss how to speak affirming words in Chapter 6.)

Making eye-contact is a great technique to use when you want to reconnect with someone. If you're a parent, try to incorporate it into your everyday routine:

- When your kid walks into the room, stop what you're doing, look at them, and let them know you are happy to see them.

- Before they walk out the door in the morning, pause, look at them for 30 seconds, and say, "I love you. I believe in you. And no matter what, I am *for* you."

- At the dinner table, look into their eyes as they talk about their day.

- When you see them off to bed or tuck them in at night, make eye contact as you say goodnight and offer encouragement.

## Connect Through Touch

Tone of voice and eye contact are incredible on their own, but connecting through appropriate physical touch is a powerful way to let kids know you are engaged and listening to them. When someone starts sharing that they are hurting it's a natural reaction to try to draw closer to them physically. Touching them on the shoulder, holding their hand, and hugging from the side communicate you are ready to listen to what they have to say next. These gestures convey it's safe to keep talking without even saying a word.

Parents, have you ever tried holding your kid when they are emotional? Sure, their instinct might be to push you away, but if they will allow you (not forced) to hold them, what tends to happen is that eventually, they will let the floodgates open and release all the emotions they've been holding inside.

**An important note:** When using tools like eye contact and appropriate physical touch, make sure you're aware of how the child is responding. If they seem uncomfortable, you may need to change your approach. Every child is different, and some may not respond positively to eye contact and/or appropriate physical touch.

## Mirror What They Say

If you've gotten this far and have been successful in getting a kid or teen to open up by mostly holding your tongue, you can help keep things going by acknowledging what they are saying and letting them know what you are hearing. In his book *Getting the Love You Want*, Harville Hendrix introduces the "Couples Dialogue." Even though his intention was to focus on couples, the same principles can be used in communicating with kids and teenagers.[30]

He suggests that we respond first with mirroring what we hear, then validating and showing empathy for what the speaker is expressing. It might sound like this:

"So, what you are saying is . . ."
"I can understand how you would feel that way."
"I can imagine you might feel _____."

When you respond in ways that seek to understand what they are feeling, you show that you are listening on a deeper level.

## Avoid Clichés

Just as it's important to have a few go-to responses, it is important to *avoid* a few. There's nothing that makes someone feel unheard, dismissed, and unseen than to throw out unhelpful clichés or quick fixes.

This reminds me of the time I (Will) was walking backwards and turned around, accidently hitting my head on a metal pole. The impact was so strong, it knocked me out. When I woke up, a man who witnessed it was standing over me. He asked the most ridiculously sounding question in that moment,

"Did that hurt?"

"No, Chuck. It tickled," I responded facetiously.

We all say dumb things in the worst moments sometimes, so I can't be too hard on his efforts to make sure I was okay. But when we are listening to someone who is deeply hurting, it's important to avoid certain statements or questions we tend to use when we feel uncomfortable or don't know what to say. These are "filler" statements that can shut down conversations.

## CLICHÉS TO AVOID

- **"How are you?"** This question is too broad and will likely not promote conversation.

- **"This is no big deal."** This is another example of dismissing like we discussed in Chapter Four. The person in crisis is the only one who can determine the degree of crisis.

- **"You should see what I have to deal with."** By the nature of this cliché, you are making it about you, not about listening.

- **"You'll get over this."** This statement lacks empathy and doesn't promote the decrease of right-brain energy and thoughts.

- **"How do you think you are making your Mom / Dad / friend feel?"** This can create a feeling of guilt and shame. The reasoning goes something like this, I feel bad ➜ I'm causing my loved one to feel bad ➜ I feel shame and guilt ➜ There must be something wrong with me.

- **"Don't cry."** This is dismissive and further suppresses the emotions.

- **"Everything happens for a reason."** Or, when someone is grieving, **"Heaven gained another angel."** Responses like these can be dismissive and not helpful for those in despair.

- "Why" questions, like, **"Why did this happen?"** Or, **"Why do I feel this way?"** Remember that sometimes there is no explanation. Just listen.

- Timelines, like **"You'll be over this in no time."** Or, **"It will be hard for a few months, but you'll feel better soon."** This can create unrealistic expectations. Though we should always have hope and believe they will heal and overcome, we shouldn't place an expectation of the timeline of that healing. We have no idea how long it will take.

Listening well communicates you care. The more you practice listening in the everyday moments, the better you get at listening in the crucial moments. (You won't have to keep thinking about what you are going to say next.) Listening is an art you can learn using the tools we've already talked about. So, work hard at it.

Let's review what we've learned so far. We start the pairing process that heals despair by first showing up. This allows us to see our kids more fully and helps them to emotionally exhale. When we listen carefully to what they are feeling, they feel safe and understood. This gives us an amazing opportunity to use the next tool and deposit little gifts into their soul.

## APPLICATION EXERCISES
How Can I Apply This Tool?

1. Practice "Tell me more" statements. A "Tell me more" posture gives the other person the platform, shows them you are interested in what they are saying, and it gives them a safe place to continue to emotionally exhale.

2. Use active listening responses like:

   "So, what you are saying is . . ."

   "I can understand how you would feel that way."

   "I can imagine you might feel _____."

3. Increase eye-contact when listening and use appropriate physical touch. The brain responds in predictable ways through healthy attachment. Eye contact and *appropriate* physical touch can reassure a kid or teen who is in despair that they are safe.

   Appropriate physical touch looks different for a parent than for another caring adult, such as a coach or small group leader. For a parent, appropriate physical touch can look like a hug, touching their arm, or holding their hands. For a caring adult, all physical touch may not be appropriate. However, usually a touch on the shoulder or a hug is okay. Caring adults helping a kid or teen in despair should remember that any appropriate touch should be given *with consent and in public* with other adults present.

# SIX
# SPEAK LIFE

## MEET HALLE

I (Chinwé) met Halle when she was 16. Halle was a stunning high school junior who appeared to have so much going for her. She was smart, inquisitive, creative, and had a close relationship with her family. When I walked out to the office lobby to meet Halle, I was immediately struck by her confidence as she stood up and firmly shook my hand. I remember wondering if she had taken any ballet classes as she seemed to almost glide across the room and onto the sofa. Halle exuded poise and self-control. She jumped into the conversation by sharing her goals for therapy and then quickly rattled off all the extracurricular activities she was involved in and how each would benefit her at the colleges she had been researching since the sixth grade. Halle was musically and athletically talented, and she had lots of friends.

*Wow,* I thought. If any teen were solidly navigating the murky waters of adolescence, it was surely Halle. On the surface, that seemed accurate, but about fifteen minutes into our session, I realized the opposite was true.

Future sessions revealed that Halle was not at all the confident person her façade seemed to suggest. Instead, she was plagued by an onslaught of critical self-talk and driven by performance-based acceptance.

"I am a slow internal processor," she would say. "I am the least talented person on the volleyball team." "I am not very smart; I just work hard."

The negative self-appraisals were ongoing. "My friends only pretend to like me; they just tolerate me." "I am not good enough."

When I would attempt to refute her harsh assessment, she would remark, "Thanks, Dr. Chinwé, but, really, I am actually below average."

What seemed to confound her most was that she couldn't point to anything that made her feel that way. "It's not like I had any terrible things happen to me," she said, alluding to what many believe, that you can only feel despair if you have a history of trauma.

I knew from years of clinical experience this false perception only exacerbated feelings of confusion and shame.

While Halle had a very loving and supportive home environment, like many girls I have counseled, Halle's pain centered around relationships. She had been ridiculed and ostracized by her "friend group" in middle school and since then struggled to navigate the cascade of critical messages that bombarded her from society (her peers).

## Affirm Kids Constantly

Because of the barrage of critical and accusatory voices that echo around our teenagers, it is vital for parents and other caring adults to constantly speak affirming words to kids in every phase of life—words that build and speak life. People frequently talk about speaking life into kids, but what does it actually mean? Speaking life means to intentionally encourage kids by using words that are fruitful, purposeful, and positive.

Negative words quickly turn into negative thoughts which can be both damaging and self-perpetuating.

A kid needs to hear many more positive comments to counteract the negative ones. The reason lies in the way that our brains are wired. Due to what's called the brain's *negativity bias,* the human brain does not perceive positive words as a threat to survival; therefore, it does not respond as quickly as it does to negative words.[31]

Think of the brain like the stomach. Not knocking on sugar, but we all know the positive and negative aspects of sugar. Negative words act a lot like sugar. They process quickly, get into the bloodstream and ultimately turn into an extra five pounds we carry around. Positive words are more like fiber. They're good for us, but our bodies don't process them as quickly.

Negative words and thoughts have much more impact on us than positive ones. They are quicker to surface and harder to disconfirm. In other words, negative words get into our bloodstream faster and stick around longer.

The strategy to combat the effect of negativity is to overwhelm it with positive affirmation, through repetition. Researchers suggest that we generate at least three positive comments or feelings for each negative expression.[32] The optimal range is five positive comments and thoughts to each negative one. Repeated affirmation builds hope.

Kids and teens need hope. They need to know their life holds immense value, despite their imperfections and what the world says about them. God has placed unique attributes within each of us that reflect His very nature—who He is. To capitalize on their inherent strengths, kids need to know who they are and *whose they are*, and who they are **not**.

Despair has a way of making them lose hope and lean more into who they are not.

One of the most fulfilling aspects of my work as a counselor is being able to *speak life* into young people. I love to praise their brilliance and celebrate both their present virtues and future contributions. I find that the clients that benefit the most have parents who are doing the same thing—at least most of the time.

Parents, teachers, and leaders must deliberately, purposefully, and clearly, speak life into kids. The simple act of speaking life is powerful and can be transformative in the life of a child. When affirming your kid or teen, keep in mind the following tips:

Keep it simple,
keep it specific,
and leave an impact.

Impact is felt with repetition over time.

## A Call to Fathers

If you are the father of a kid or teen, please know that you play an enormous role in the life of your daughter or son. Your words will shape their destiny and have a long-lasting impact.

If you are the father of a daughter, I have a special request of you: Affirm your daughters. Not just by words and gestures, but by intentional and consistent actions that send the message you are there for them. The research is clear. Fathers play a pivotal role in their daughter's self-image, self-esteem, and body image. Studies also show that girls with close and affirming relationships with their fathers are more likely to have self-confidence, perform better academically and have more successful career advancement.[33]

## Spark Purpose and Passion

So, how do you speak life to a kid or teen when despair has sunk in and there is very little that resembles life?

Our kids have gifts they have yet to realize. But that's just it; they don't realize it. We lead our children by speaking God's word and His truths into their lives. And while doing so, it's important to focus on character and not performance. Kids and teens need to see that we love them for who they are—not what they are doing. Halle struggled so much with her identity that most of what she did became performative.

Encourage someone in the present while giving them hope for the future. You offer hope by calling out their seeds of greatness and declaring God's blessings over them.

To that end, tone, eye contact, and intentionality matter more than ever. (See chapters three and four.)

Not sure where to start? Encourage them by saying things like:

- "I am proud of you."
- "You are amazing."
- "You are smart."
- "You are talented."
- "You will do amazing things in this life."

Also, remind them to whom they belong by stating things, like:

- "You are a child of God."
- "You already have victory."
- "I believe God is going to do some amazing things in your life, and there are good days ahead."
- "You are fearfully and wonderfully made."

When you speak life-giving or hopeful words to your kids, you are enabling them to *reframe beliefs* about themselves. When you flood them with words that build them up, you breathe new life into them, and remind them of their worth. You are also giving them a source they can tap into when they feel deflated—a deep well of truth that enables them to speak life to themselves so that they can claim their worth.

**Did you know that speaking positively to yourself can change the way your brain is wired? Our brain *really* can change.**

Scientists once believed the brain is hardwired at birth. Brain researchers have long disputed that notion. Spanning several decades of neuroscientific research, we now know that the brain is plastic, meaning it can adapt both physically and chemically given the proper conditions.[34]

Changing our minds enables our brains to change. Indeed, we can actually change the structure of our brain by the thoughts we most consistently think. Cognitive neuroscientist Dr. Caroline Leaf wrote in her book *Switch on Your Brain: The Key to Peak Happiness, Thinking, and Health*:

> "Thoughts are real, physical things that occupy mental real estate. Moment by moment, every day, you are changing the structure of your brain through your thinking. When we hope, it is an activity of the mind that changes the structure of our brain in a positive and normal direction."[35]

The title of their book *Words Can Change Your Brain* certainly says it all, because neuroscientist Dr. Andrew Newberg and communications expert Marc Robert Waldman wrote, "a single word has the power to influence the expression of genes . . ." The authors are considered two of the world's leading experts in spirituality and the brain. Their research shows that it is actually quite simple (in fact it takes less than a minute) to retrain one's brain to communicate with greater compassion. Words such as "peace" and "love" can actually turn on stress-reducing genes.[36] In other words, words matter. Words don't change reality, but they can change how the youth in our lives perceive reality.

Modern scientific evidence connects our thoughts to how we perceive ourselves and others. But if you go way back to approximately 57 A.D., the apostle Paul gave us biblical instruction on the significance of our thoughts and the importance of renewing our minds: "Do not conform to the pattern of this world, but be transformed by the renewing of your mind. Then you will be able to test and approve what God's will is—his good, pleasing and perfect will" (Romans 12:12, NIV).

This renewal that Paul points out centers on the acceptance of our new identity in Christ based on significance, security, and hope—hope that we receive from our relationship with Christ, as well as our connection with others. Teaching our kids and teens how to respond to negative self-talk makes a big difference in how they feel—not just in the moment but over time.

In Halle's story, negative words were spoken to her that left her feeling unworthy and inferior. These critical thoughts later shaped her perception and relationship with others and herself. Over time, Halle began to internalize these thoughts, which caused her to interpret many situations in unhelpful ways.

The foundation of who Halle is in Christ had already been laid (with the help of her parents and other Christian leaders in her life). But as she journeyed through childhood and adolescence, regrettably, she lost sight of who she is, and she began to believe lies about herself. The recovery process for Halle required her to lean into her true identity in Christ. Over time, and with the help of those who loved her, she eventually learned how to take hold of her thoughts, replacing the critical, internal voices with life-giving truths.

I wish I could say that Halle got better right away, but it took time. Through the hard work of retraining her thoughts, and with the tremendous support of her parents through some very dark days, I am pleased to share that Halle has now adopted the attitude of being fully approved.

## Get Rid of the Ants

Have you ever associated unsettling thoughts with little pesky ants crawling around your brain? Well, Dr. Daniel Amen has. I (Chinwé) am a huge fan of Dr. Amen's name (pretty cool, right?) and even more impressed with his work. Dr. Amen is a clinical neuroscientist and psychiatrist. He tells a story about a time when he was in medical school, coming home frustrated and tired after a long day of working with patients with complex, depressive disorders.

He was ready to kick his shoes off and relax only to discover thousands of ants crawling around his kitchen. He fumed at the added aggravation of cleaning up the swarm of ants, and he began thinking of it in the context of the patients he'd just treated that day. It was as if ants had been crowding and taking over their brains—just like the infestation occurring in his kitchen! That's how an acronym was born: **A**utomatic **N**egative **T**houghts (ANTs).[37] He then began teaching his patients how to get rid of all of the ANTs that were robbing them of peace and joy.

According to some scientists, we have an estimated 6,200 thoughts run through our minds *per* day.[38] Thoughts are plentiful and powerful. For instance, did you know that every time you think a thought, your brain releases chemical energy? When those thoughts become overly critical, hopeless, or judgmental, the released chemicals initiate physiological responses in the body: heart rate increases, muscles become tense, and breathing becomes shallow. Negative thinking over a long period of time damages the brain, leading to a low attention span, poor judgement, and memory problems.[39]

Like so many bad cycles we can get caught up in, persistent negative thoughts can be habit-forming. They rewrite the brain and reinforce existing neural pathways, making it much more likely that the kid or teen you love will nurse those pessimistic glass-half-empty thoughts. The detrimental impact of those thoughts goes well beyond mental and emotional health.

According to the *Journal of the American Medical Association* (JAMA), close to 80 percent of all diseases are initiated and exacerbated by stress.[40] The relationship between stress and mental illnesses is stronger than the relationship between stress and physical illnesses.[41] *The American Institute of Stress* estimates 75-90 percent of all primary care visits are for stress-related reasons.[42] Many of the clients I've counseled over the years have inaccurately attributed persistent stomach or body aches or chronic fatigue to a disease they were certain they had. They were surprised to learn that frequent critical thoughts can lead to chronic stress and serious, physical health issues.

ANTs, left to roam, can make us very ill. To a greater or lesser extent, we all occasionally experience ANTs that we are able to fumigate effectively. However, when despair surfaces, fumigation becomes much more difficult, but it's not impossible.

## Challenge Negative Thoughts

We all know what it's like to be plagued by unhealthy, unkind, and unwanted thoughts. Prolonged negative thinking can create neural pathways in the brain that can decrease motivation and initiate sadness, but there is good news! A number of studies show that challenging negative thoughts effectively reduces stress, improves mood, and decreases the risk of physical illnesses.[43]

Often, simply bringing attention to an ANT will be enough to exterminate it, but, for deeply ingrained thoughts that have become a core belief, it will require some extra effort. That is when you have to do the work of retraining your brain.

When a negative thought arises, I teach my clients to exterminate them using a cognitive restructuring strategy that I adapted from a Socratic Questioning[44] method called THINK. You can try this at home or in a small group with your kid or teen.

A simple strategy to help your kid or teen evaluate unhealthy and unhelpful thought patterns and disrupt the negative thought cycle is to encourage them to THINK.

Is this thought **T**rue?

Is it **H**elpful?

Is it **I**nspiring?

Is it **N**ecessary?

Is it **K**ind?

I like the THINK strategy because it temporarily forces kids and teenagers to disengage with the emotional part of the brain and re-engage with the frontal lobe, a more logical and rational part of the brain.

## T — Is It True?

A brain in despair is extremely compelling. It convinces us that all of the hardships in life (difficult break-ups, global warming, a health pandemic) are the result of our poor choices. It especially convinces teenagers or kids that they "can never get anything right." If your child or teen expresses this, help them learn to refute the lies they may be believing with truths.

| NEGATIVE STATEMENT | BALANCED STATEMENT |
|---|---|
| I'm such a failure. | Yes, I make mistakes, but overall, I make good choices. |
| | |
| | |
| | |
| | |
| | |

## H — Is It Helpful?

Stress and overthinking are a common symptom of an anxious or depressed brain. Something small and insignificant can keep us up half the night operating under the false assumption, "If I think about it a lot, a solution will come." Let's bust a myth: Overthinking a problem rarely generates a solution; instead, it elevates anxiety. According to a study done at Cornell University, 85 percent of what we worry about never occurs, so, overthinking is not helpful![45]

For young people who tend to ruminate (constantly worrying about the past or the future), this one simple strategy may help. Ask them to worry for an entire day and then right before bed, assess what percentage of the time worrying led to problem-solving. Typically, it is a very low percentage, so instead, encourage your student to set a timer for 10 minutes and write down all of the things worrying them and possible solutions. After the timer goes off, present that list to a friend or trusted adult to brainstorm other potential solutions. If you happen to be the trusted adult they consult, help them to redirect their thoughts by asking them, "What other ways can you view this issue?"

| WORRIES | POSSIBLE SOLUTIONS |
|---|---|
| | |
| | |
| | |
| | |

## I — Is It Inspiring?

The negative, inner critic is less than inspiring or uplifting. It loves to speak in absolutes. In fact, our brains were designed for mental shortcuts. Therefore, any belief that is stated in absolutes is easily embraced. Critical statements such as, "I will never get anything right" and "I will always be a failure" are the mainstays of a brain in despair.

When you hear these rigid statements, seek out the exception and use yourself as an example. "Well, I have made many mistakes. Does that mean I will always be a disappointment or a failure?" Help them to eliminate two of the most beloved words of a brain in despair: "always" and "never."

## N — Is It Necessary?

In his book *Meditations*, Stoic philosopher Marcus Aurelius wrote, "Most of what we say and do is not necessary, and its omission would save both time and trouble."[46] This also applies to what we think.

Out of the 6,200 thoughts our human brain generates, 80 percent of them are negative and 95 percent are repeated thoughts from the previous day. Much of what we think about is negative, superfluous, or repetitive. Because the mind's tendency is to focus on unfounded fears and worries, it is important to learn the skill of taking a step back and evaluating the thoughts that arise. With every self-critical thought, encourage your kid or teen to ask themselves if it is necessary.

|  | YES | NO |
|---|---|---|
| Is this thought repetitive? |  |  |
| Is it excessive? |  |  |
| Is it improving the situation? |  |  |

If the answer is NO, it's unnecessary, so let's think of another thought instead.

## K — Is It Kind?

Self-compassion involves speaking to yourself kindly as you would to a dear friend who is suffering. Kids and teenagers suffering with depression or despair often struggle with self-compassion because the mind in despair has them believing they are unworthy of kindness or care.

Self-compassion is the very last thing they will want to do, but it really does help. Encourage them to think about what they might say to a friend or a small child in the same situation. What would they say? Replacing self-criticism with self-compassion will lead to increased acceptance over time.

| THINGS I SAY TO MYSELF | THINGS I SAY TO A FRIEND |
|---|---|
| | |
| | |
| | |

Like anything worth doing, implementing the THINK technique becomes easier with time and practice. While aspects of our natural thinking patterns can be challenging—particularly when in despair—helping our kids and teenagers develop skills to master their mindset can result in a positive state of mind, increased inner strength (grit), and resilience.

## APPLICATION EXERCISES
How Can I Apply This Tool?

1. Speak more words of life to your kids and teens more often. Tell them you love them. Tell them you are proud of them. Write sticky notes and leave them on their bathroom mirror or locker at school. When birthdays come around, write a card with substance. Keep speaking and leaving notes even if it feels like it doesn't make a difference. It does!

2. The Bible indicates that "life and death are in the power of the tongue (Proverbs 18:21)." As parents and caring adults, we can both positively and negatively influence kids' lives by our words. Emphasize scriptural truths that speak hope into your kid or teen. Here are some examples . . .

   a. You were lovingly and intentionally created by God. (Psalm 139:14)

   b. God has a special plan for your life. (Jeremiah 29:11)

   c. God is always with you. (Deuteronomy 31:6)

3. Faithfully speaking truths will help them to establish their identity in Christ. In addition . . .

   ■ Encourage them by sharing your observations of their efforts rather than solely offering praise for their appearance or abilities. For example, "I noticed that you shared part of your lunch with a friend who forgot his at home," or, "I can tell that you've been putting in some extra hours on the ball field this week in preparation for the game," and, "I noticed you listened respectfully even when you didn't agree with my viewpoint."

   ■ Be direct and honest. Why? Kids and teens, in particular, are really good at detecting fabrications. You establish credibility with them when you always tell them the truth.

   ■ Avoid criticizing your kid or teen publicly. This is shaming and damages your relationship with your child.

# SEVEN
# BUILD GRIT

I (Chinwé) will never forget my first counseling position as a high school counselor. The school where I worked was unique. It served a racially and economically diverse student body ranging from kids residing in low-income communities to those from some of the wealthiest families in the city. I was 23 years old when I started, just three years older than the oldest enrolled high school senior. Leading at such a young age presented more than a few challenges but many more advantages. I could relate to many of my students' struggles, being not far removed from those very same battles.

## MEET IMANI AND DAYNA

I know this is a cliché, but as a junior counselor, I truly learned a great deal more from my students than I could ever have taught them. When I reflect on that time and the lessons I learned, two student-athletes immediately come to mind. Let's call one Imani and the other Dayna. They each showed up in the counseling suite with a similar look of tearful shock mixed with devastation. Neither of them made the girls' basketball team after playing varsity the year before. The team had recruited several talented student-athletes, and try-outs for that year were exponentially more competitive than in previous years. This news was shattering to both girls, who played different positions but were equally talented in their own right. Both expressed disappointment, exclusion, and anxiety about their future in basketball.

After two weeks of counseling, I noticed a contrast in each girls' disposition and behavior. While still disappointed, Imani felt empowered and was determined to work hard during the year and try out the following season. Dayna, however, decided that she wasn't "cut out for basketball." Dayna, a life-long athlete, did not play any sport for the remainder of high school and later battled serious self-esteem issues. Imani made the varsity team the following year and ultimately secured an athletic scholarship to a Division I college.

I grew increasingly fascinated by their stories. Both had endured the same setback, and both perceived the experience as a "failure." But each student responded in completely opposite ways. I often wondered, *What led Imani to persevere and bounce back from adversity, while Dayna seemed to give up?*

Similar questions emerged in my work with *other* students:

*How is it that kids who grew up in difficult or sometimes traumatic life conditions—neglect, abuse, and abandonment—appear not just to survive but thrive, often academically exceeding kids who came from the most affluent and well-connected families in the city?*

Thirty years of collective scientific research combined with my years of clinical work has provided the answer to those questions: **Resilience.**

We also like to refer to it as GRIT. Angela Duckworth, the nation's leading expert on grit, did a fantastic job of defining grit through years of research:

"Grit is passion and sustained persistence applied toward long-term achievement."[47]

What makes grit particularly fascinating is that youth who have grit feel empowered to keep going and going and going, with little preoccupation with or concern for rewards or personal recognition along the way.

Grit is a combination of resilience, ambition, and self-control in the pursuit of a goal that can take months or even decades to achieve. Similar to resilience, grit involves adapting to or bouncing back from adversity, which is the ability to positively adjust under extremely challenging life conditions—such as the loss of a loved one, financial strain or poverty, or a serious health issue or illness.[48]

The simple fact is that no matter who you are or where you come from, bad things will happen. The apostle John states, "In this world, we will have trouble" (John 16:33, NIV). We've all experienced challenges and adversity, either first-hand or indirectly.

Knowing that adversity will always be a part of our kids' lives and teaching them how to respond by embracing—not resisting—the lessons discovered as they maneuver through adversity are two key components to battling despair.[49]

If you are reading this and wondering if resilience or grit is something only certain kids with specific personalities possess, or if you are feeling doubtful that your kid or teen can activate this "gene" or develop this trait, please know this:

All kids and teens are capable of resilience and grit. These are skills that can be *nurtured* by the important adults in their life. Those nurturing experiences can help to not only change your youth's thinking but also help them to feel empowered to tackle many of life's most difficult challenges.

Practically speaking, how can you, as a parent or youth leader or grandparent or teacher, help a kid or teen develop grit and resilience? Here are some ideas:

## Prepare for Trouble and Reframe

It's important to note that being resilient does not keep stress at bay. Rather, the *grittiest* and most resilient people have seen their share of heartache and commonly experience distress.

Gritty individuals understand that stress is a part of life and is not always a negative thing. In fact, stress enables young people to discover within themselves the gears or strategies they didn't know they had but that are necessary to tackle life's obstacles.

As caring adults, we must teach kids and teens to accept change and disappointment as part of the human experience. We can help them to understand that, yes, many life circumstances are outside of their control but that they have control over how they react to those circumstances.

Studies show that optimism and flexibility are linked to resilience.[50,51] Some optimism is genetic, whereas some aspects can be learned. For example, the ability to reframe negative events is linked to resilience. Reframing is a strategy often used by therapists to help clients look at situations from a different perspective. During times of disappointment or loss, reframing helps kids focus on the things they have, rather than on what was lost. Reframing reminds kids to focus less on what is outside of one's control but on those things that can be modified, such as our thoughts and perceptions.[52]

Here's an example of how to build this skill in a younger kid:

> **Disappointing event**: A playdate was canceled due to inclement weather.
>
> **Child reacts**: He feels rejected, withdraws, is disappointed, and even angry.
>
> **Parent responds**: "I can understand how bummed you are about your playdate getting canceled. I know how much you were looking forward to playing with

Malcolm today. I would be sad also. Maybe we can look at this experience a little differently."

**Parent continues**: "What is it that we get to do that we may not have been able to do if the weather had been nice?" (Younger children or a child who is very upset will need your help coming up with some ideas.)

"We could go to the bookstore and get a new book for your library. We could also watch a new movie, or schedule a tea party, or have a mega Lego® challenge. What do you think? Do you have any other fun ideas?"

For tweens or teens, the situation could look like this:

**Disappointing event**: A senior just discovered he didn't get into his top-choice dream school he's been working toward, taking multiple AP classes since freshman year.

**Teen reacts**: He feels rejected, withdraws, is disappointed, and angry. He wonders out loud, "Am I just not good enough?"

**Parent responds**: "I can understand how disappointed you are about this. You've envisioned yourself at this school for a long time, and you've been working so hard to meet all of the admissions requirements. I would be very upset also."

**Parent continues after a few minutes**: "That was a highly competitive school. And, you've received acceptances from the other four schools that were on your list. There's no perfect school. Realistically, what are the chances that one of those other schools on your list might *also* offer a great education and be an even better fit for your specific major and personality?" or, "Didn't you mention that Stacey decided to attend one of those schools? What about reaching out to her to see what led to her decision?"

When the teen feels ready, help him or her to brain-storm some actions that they can take such as researching potential graduate programs at their dream school, or viewing attendance at one of the other schools as a blessing in disguise.

My years as a counselor have shown me that parents play an important role in helping kids and teens develop a critical life skill following disappointment: acknowledging one's feelings and then taking a step back to view the bigger picture with more balanced thinking. Steering kids *away* from looking at what they have lost and *towards* the opportunities that have now been presented helps build resilience and grit.

## Be a Safe Person

Kids and teens undergo tremendous changes as they are developing—physical, social, and emotional. And as they grapple with the peaks and valleys of life, they will inevitably experience stress and even adversity. Research suggests that the presence of at least one safe adult helps lead kids through adversity.[53] In almost any situation, particularly with younger kids, you will serve as your child's emotional barometer. Any adult in the life of a child or teen (parent, small group leader, coach, or teacher) can strengthen their ability to endure life's inevitable challenges simply by being a *safe person*.

But what makes a person feel safe?

Safety encompasses not just physical or environmental safety but also emotional safety. When kids are younger, their world is very small and well-defined (home, grandma's house, the park, daycare, and maybe LegoLand®). Safety centers on a reliable and predictable routine and the adults in their life showing up when they say they will. As kids get older, safety looks a little different. More people and places are introduced and more questions surface.

Middle and high schoolers are grappling with more complex, and sometimes global issues. While some are really good at hiding their need for emotional safety, it is especially critical for teens. When teens share that scary thing about themselves or their friends, your response matters. During a difficult life event, responding with calmness, empathy, and validation helps reverse the physiological effects of prolonged distress.

Finally, safety does not equate to initiating a rescue mission. As parents, when we see our kids stumble, fall, or experience intense fear, our instinct is to jump in and fix it. It's natural, but the problem is, it isn't helpful. In the short-term, it might reduce their anxiety (and ours), but it does not allow the opportunity for those important, life-coping skills to develop. Helping your kid or teen learn to manage their anxiety and distress without parental intervention will help them build the grit necessary to feel more confident and in control—both now and as an adult.

## Highlight Current Strengths and Past Victories

While disappointments are an inevitable part of life, they can be intensely disheartening for a kid or teen already battling despair. The negativity bias associated with a brain in despair will be quick to pull up countless examples of past failures and seemingly impossible future hurdles. That's because despair has a pesky way of amplifying negative messages and fading out the positive ones.

This is where you come in. While you did not cause the problem of despair, the good news is that you can be a part of the solution. Reminding kids of their character strengths and past successes is a helpful way to build confidence and resilience. Whether individually or in a small group setting, be the cheering fan club that consistently points out the barriers your teen in despair has overcome. Highlighting their current strengths and past victories serves as a reminder of what they were once able to bounce back from—and can do again.

## Foster a Growth Mindset

The goal of every adult should be to influence kids who have the confidence to set and achieve challenging (not just safe) goals that will successfully carry them through to adulthood; however, it is not easy for a kid in despair to recover from a major, emotional setback. The urge to move on, or *avoid* difficult emotions or situations, can be hard to resist. However, a kid with grit learns to push through disappointment. Remember Dayna, who lost her spot on the basketball team? None of us blamed Dayna for *feeling* like giving up in the face of what seemed to be a tremendously painful rejection. Being only human, she did what many of us would have done or thought about doing at that age.

Dayna didn't realize two crucial truths that we now know from research:

1. It isn't the event itself but our response to setbacks that help shape our attitudes and next steps.

2. Learning from failure is an essential path towards future success and an essential component of resilience and grit.

Embracing failure is a hard pill for any of us to swallow, but actively limiting new experiences results in fewer risks being taken by our kids and teens, and consequently, fewer opportunities for growth.

Numerous studies conclude that resilience, or grit, is an emotional muscle that can be strengthened.[54, 55] One tool that helps a kid or teen override the fear of failure and strengthen that critical muscle is adopting a growth mindset. The growth mindset, a term developed by Stanford University psychologist Carol Dweck, is the belief that our abilities can develop with practice, feedback, and effort.[56]

Similar to grit, kids with a growth mindset put in the effort required to achieve a goal. Stick-to-itiveness is the hallmark of a growth mindset. As Thomas A. Edison once said, *"I have not failed. I've just found 10,000 ways that won't work."* This idea connects to despair.

Just as we reframe the way we think about disappointments, we can help our young people reframe how they view failure, not as something to be desperately avoided, but as a developmental process. Kids and teens (like Imani) who adopt a growth mindset are likely to try again once they have failed at something, taking steps towards figuring out new ways to improve and succeed, thus hopefully circumventing despair.

As the adults who desire to empower them, our role is to remind kids and teens that they can overcome hard things and consistently point out when they make an effort to push through—not bypass—something challenging. We all need to be reminded that sustained effort eventually leads to success. Sustained effort over time is a demonstration of grit.

## Talk About the Climb

As a therapist, the "pressure to succeed" burdens many of the kids I (Chinwe) meet. For most of the girls I counsel, this pressure extends to all areas. While this pressure is often fueled from within, caring adults sometimes play a role unwittingly. Many parents and leaders aren't always cognizant of the messages they send to kids about what it means to be successful and what we believe about those who miss the mark. Kids are inundated with conflicting, and often misguided, messages about their self-worth and future potential from peers, media, and sometimes even the adults who love them.

And as it relates to this idea of "success," many adults experience doubt and insecurities about their own journeys, which are often reflected in the retelling of their victory stories. No matter how difficult an experience has been, some of us tend to focus on the successful parts of the story and frequently dismiss or overlook those turbulent weeks, months, or even years spent toiling towards the finish line.

Keeping in mind their developmental age and maturity, it's helpful to allow kids and teens to see and hear how you've dealt with adversity. Share your life experiences and not just the highlight reel. Dig down for those stories that live in the valley *before sharing* the ones about the subsequent climb. Allowing a peek into your own challenging life experiences and all of the emotions that came alongside them, helps kids and teens understand that frustration, sadness, and even a bit of mild despair are expected in this life. Then after you share, be sure to encourage them to ask questions about what it was like for you to be in the pit and what you learned, not just when you reached the top, but as you struggled to climb out.

If the thought of having this conversation evokes some discomfort, take some time to consider your own feelings about success, failure, and adversity. Here are some questions for self-reflection:

- How do you define success? How did you define success as a child?

- Where did that definition of success originate?

- Did you excel in academics, the arts, or athletics? How did you define success in those areas?

- How do you describe your own adversity? Do you think of your failures as negatives or opportunities for growth?

## Balance Support with Challenge

Some things kids can do quite well on their own, while other things will require the help of the adults who love them. This is the reason building grit is a critical connection tool. My (Chinwé) husband Lonnie and my son Brayden frequently bond through activities. When Brayden received his first jigsaw puzzle, initially, we allowed him to try putting it together on his own.

Unsurprisingly, he struggled and became frustrated. Lonnie then sat patiently with him, describing simple strategies, beginning with locating all the corner pieces first. With support and encouragement (and still occasional frustration), Brayden learned how to solve the puzzle and many more complicated puzzles that followed.

Much of my understanding about the process of learning comes from the work of Lev Vygotsky, considered the father of social developmental theory. Vygotsky's theory highlights the role of supportive people in a kid's life as fundamental to learning. The zone of proximal development is a primary principle of Vygotsky's work, which is defined as the difference between what a kid or teen can achieve independently and what is necessary to accomplish with the support of a skilled teacher (often a parent, but can also be a youth pastor or a coach). [57]

While it may be tempting to give in to your middle-schooler's daily tantrums or your high-schooler's request to complete his English essay for him, the longer-term consequences may be harsher. The effective "teacher" (you) balances support with challenge. The student (your kid or teen) then internalizes the information and uses it to guide his or her own performance. The takeaway is this: As our kids become more competent, they become more confident. This confidence fuels a desire to work more independently and creatively. Over time, your role as a teacher decreases. Providing your kid or teen ample opportunities to think and behave independently helps to build their psychological fitness and emotional grit.

When kids and teens understand that you are encouraging them to succeed and rooting for them through life's hurdles, it enhances their sense of attachment and security. In other words, they feel connected and empowered.

It is also important to remember that healing from despair often comes from small but consistent changes in thinking, feeling, and doing. Focusing on these resilience and grit tools will empower young people so they can better navigate difficult life situations while simultaneously growing to be confident in who God designed them to be—an overcomer.

# APPLICATION EXERCISES
## How Can I Apply This Tool?

1. Remind kids and teens of their past successes. This is a helpful way to build confidence and resilience. Whether individually or in a small group setting, be the cheering fan club that consistently points out the barriers your teen in despair has overcome.

2. Call out character traits you see in kids such as, courage, consistency, love, humility, strength, compassion, honesty, and determination. Point out their work ethic, perseverance, and resolve under pressure. Be sure to highlight specific examples that you and others have observed in this regard.

3. Focus on building competence and confidence. As kids and teens become more competent, they feel more confident. Providing your kid or teen ample opportunities to think and behave independently helps to build their emotional grit. Increase self-sufficiency by encouraging everyday decisions (e.g., agreeing on curfews, applying for a summer job, or choosing which college to attend). Foster confidence by allowing space for independent and responsible decision-making skills to develop, but remain a sounding board for your kid or teen.

4. Here's a four-part, decision-making strategy that can help guide them when faced with a tough decision:

   ❶ Is it safe?
   ❷ Have I gathered all of the relevant information?
   ❸ Does it align with my values?
   ❹ Who do I need to consult with about this?

Once a final decision has been made, be genuinely excited for them and yourself. You are raising and/or leading a self-sufficient and resilient kid or teen!

# EIGHT

# THERE IS ALWAYS HOPE

I (Will) had just finished a school assembly for 900 middle school students when John walked up to me. "Excuse me, Will. Do you have time to talk to my friend Hannah?" John pointed to the bleachers where three other students were consoling a female student. As I approached the group, I was careful to take a deep breath. I had just started packing up and thinking about what was next on my schedule. But in moments like this, I knew I had to show up. Hannah was clearly upset.

I sat down next to Hannah and tried to get a sense of what she was feeling.

"I can see that you are upset. What's going on?"

Her friends began to tell me she had been struggling with insecurities and a recent difficult situation with her Dad.

"I can imagine, that is difficult. How do you feel, Hannah?"

"I don't know . . . I feel broken."

I smiled back at Hannah. "Hannah, you are not broken. You are hurt. Broken is a belief, hurt is a feeling."

"I feel hurt."

"Tell me more."

As Hannah emotionally exhaled her hurt, I just listened. Thankfully, she had a very supportive mom, counselor, and teacher who were aware of the challenges she was facing. I quickly realized that this was a moment not to intervene, but a moment to speak life into her.

One of the main points our team at *Curate Hope* communicates in school assemblies is the idea that every student has a purpose.

When Hannah finished telling more of her story, I looked her in the eyes and reminded her, "Hannah, you have a purpose, and your life matters."

"You really believe that?" she asked.

"I *know* that. In the short amount of time listening to you, I can tell you are a bright, caring, and loving person. You have friends surrounding you because you matter to them. Who you are is greater than the challenges of today, and one day it will be different. It won't always be this way, but you will always matter."

Hannah's demeanor started to change as her friends hugged her and nodded in agreement. It was as if we just spoke life into her soul again, reminding her that her purpose is greater than her circumstances.

This short little interaction wasn't the "magic moment" that healed all of Hannah's brokenness and despair. But it was a dose of medicine. It was a moment when she felt loved, understood, safe, worthy, and empowered.

Having a few connection tools to use in this situation gave me, as a leader, an opportunity to be a part of Hannah's journey towards healing. Along with her parents, counselor, teachers, and caring adults, I played a small part—at least that day.

Never underestimate the small moments. God often uses small interactions to initiate BIG change.

David was anointed king when Samuel poured oil over his head. Peter became a disciple when Jesus spoke two words, "Follow me." The world changed forever when Jesus spoke three words, "It is finished."

Maybe a kid's life will change the moment they know some-one is there.
Maybe a pre-teen's despair will lessen when they finally let their emotions out.
Maybe a girl in your small group will feel safe when you just listen.
Maybe your son's temptation to harm himself wanes in a moment of affirmation.
Maybe a generation of kids and teenagers can develop grit just to keep going—even when things get really tough.

We all matter in the conversation to help kids heal from despair.

Every . . .
adult,
parent,
coach,
teacher,
small group leader,
counselor,
pastor,
and mentor . . .
can offer hope.

You matter.

We must fight for **every** kid and teenager.

## This Matters.

*This matters* because since 2007 suicide rates have more than doubled among teenagers.[58] This isn't just math, these are individuals. Sons and daughters. Grandkids. Students. Friends.

*This matters* because black teenagers are experiencing high levels of despair from racial discrimination and anti-black sentiments.

*This matters* because every parent loves their kids. Every parent has dreams and hopes for their kids.

*This matters* because too many parents have wept at the deep pain from losing a child. Too many tears have been shed.

*This matters* because we have a culture that pushes down, rather than lifts up. Bullying and anonymous online bashing have become too prevalent in our culture.

*This matters* because we have a connection deficit, and isolation kills.

*This matters* because there is always hope.

Hope is our greatest weapon. We have hope that despite the brokenness of our world, love prevails more.

*This matters* because God has **not** left us alone. We have tools and ways to help encourage the brain towards healing.

When we **show up,** they feel loved.
When we **see them**, they feel understood.
When we **just listen**, they feel safe.
When we **speak life**, they feel worthy.
When we help them **develop grit**, they feel empowered.

Sometimes having the right tools can remind us about the times we've blown it. The times we've said the wrong thing or done things we regret. But the good news is, there is grace. Grace for me, and grace for you, too. We don't have to be perfect. There's no way we can get it right every time.

Please know that no matter how many times you think you've messed up, you can *still* make a difference with the kids in your life. You don't have to execute these tools perfectly in order for them to work. Each intentional decision you make *matters*. In fact, researcher John Gottman concluded that if you respond the "right way" two out of every five times, it's enough to positively influence your child's emotional state.[59]

If you're wondering what to do from here, here's what I suggest:

**Start with one.**

One tool.
One kid.
One moment.

Start today.

For additional resources,
go to TheSeenBook.com

## WHEN WE:

show up →

see them →

just listen →

speak life →

develop grit →

## THEY FEEL:

loved

understood

safe

worthy

empowered

# APPENDIX 1

## Self-Harm

Self-harm or NSSI (Non-Suicidal Self-Injury) is when an individual deliberately causes harm to themselves as a way to cope with intense emotional pain. Parents, if you aren't aware of anyone who self-harms, chances are that your teen does. While the topic of self-harming can be very alarming to parents and small group leaders, the more you know, the more you can be in the best position to recognize the signs and seek professional help.

Here's what you need to know:

- Acts of self-harm include: cutting, scratching, burning, punching things, and even hitting one's head against a wall.
- Self-harming typically stems from childhood trauma, anxiety, and depression.
- Like any other high-risk behavior (e.g., alcohol, drugs, sexual promiscuity), self-harming can be dangerous and compulsive.
- There is a misconception that young people who self-harm are attention seeking or attempting to take their own life. That is not always the case. However, all forms of self-harm should be taken seriously.

- Self-harm is usually done in secrecy as there is a great deal of stigma involved. Due to the secrecy associated with self-harming behaviors, kids and teenagers often feel guilt, shame, and a sense of isolation.

Kids and teens who self-harm are often carrying heavy burdens, and the physical pain is preferable to the emotional pain. Though it only provides momentary relief from painful emotions, the more your teen does it, the more he or she will want to do it. The reason lies in the release of endorphins, which are the "feel-good" hormones released during intense physical exertion—and also during an injury. These hormones initiate a tension-relieving sensation—also known as runner's high—hence, the habit-forming nature.

# APPENDIX 2

## Suicide Prevention

Here are some warning signs to look for when a child has suicidal thinking:

- Isolation and withdrawing from social contact, especially if it's sudden
- Being self-destructive or engaging in risk-taking behaviors
- Looking for and/or acquiring means to commit suicide, such as getting a gun or a lot of medication
- Extreme mood swings
- Frequently talking about death or dying
- Saying things like, "I wish I were dead," or, "I wish I had never been born."
- Giving away possessions for no particular reason
- Expressing hopelessness or a feeling of being trapped with no way out
- Changes in sleeping, eating, or other patterns
- Making a point to say goodbye to people
- Beginning to use alcohol and/or drugs, or using them more frequently
- Changing obvious characteristics of their personality
- Becoming extremely agitated, upset, depressed, and/or anxious

The number one suicide method used by adolescent girls is pills. Pay close attention to what access they have to pills and other possible methods.

Adolescent boys typically look for more violent methods. Once again, pay attention to resources available to them, especially if the child is facing despair.

**What to do if a kid is having suicidal thoughts:**

**Stay calm.**

This is easy to say but very hard to do because you care about the kids in your life so much. I get it. If a kid tells us they're thinking of killing themselves, our knee-jerk response, especially as parents, is to immediately start explaining to them why they shouldn't feel that way. You may make statements such as:
"You have so much to live for."
"Your life is good and you have so many people that love you."
"You have hopes and dreams."

Although it seems like this would help, it doesn't. Remember, a brain in despair cannot easily process logically. **When we approach an emotionally activated teen from a place of logic, we unintentionally reinforce their negative feelings.**

For example, it reinforces beliefs like:
"I am broken."
"There is something wrong with me."
"I shouldn't feel this way, but I do."
"The world is better off without me."
"There is no fixing it."

We've unintentionally added feelings of guilt and shame to the despair they are already facing.

Resist the urge to convince them with logic. Instead, simply meet them exactly where they are at that moment.

The best things to do and say are:
- Mirror and validate their emotions.
- Offer empathy.
- Share and express your care and love for them.
- Use attachment language such as "You are lovable" and "You can trust me to be there for you."
- Thank them for being honest with you.
- Offer to get help together.

**Get help.**

When a teenager is facing suicidal thoughts, do not navigate it alone.

For immediate help, contact the *National Suicide Prevention Hotline* by calling 1-800-273-8255 (TALK) or visiting SuicidePreventionLifeline.org. These professionals are trained to help you and your child de-escalate from a crisis moment to a place of safety and sustainability.

For ongoing help, seek out a mental health professional, like a Licensed Mental Health Counselor, who can help both you and your child in the long term.

# NOTES

1   Curtin, Sally C. M.A. and Heron, Melonie, Ph.D., "Death
    Rates Due to Suicide and Homicide Among Persons Aged
    10–24: United States, 2000–2017." CDC, National Vital
    Statistics System, October 2019, https://www.cdc.gov/
    nchs/data/databriefs/db352-h.pdf.

2   Shen K., Yang Y., Wang T., Zhao D., Jiang Y., Jin R., Zheng
    Y., Xu B., Xie Z., Lin L., Shang Y., Lu X., Shu S., Bai Y., Deng
    J., Lu M., Ye L., Wang X., Wang Y, "Diagnosis, Treatment,
    and Prevention of 2019 Novel Coronavirus Infection in
    Children: Experts' Consensus Statement," *World Journal
    of Pediatrics*: WJP;  PubMed Global Pediatric Pulmonology
    Alliance; (2020): pp. 1–9.

3   Curtin, Sally C. M.A. and Heron, Melonie, Ph.D., "Death
    Rates Due to Suicide and Homicide Among Persons Aged
    10–24."

4   Lindsey, Michael A., et al. 2019."Trends of Suicidal
    Behaviors Among High School Students in the United
    States: 1991–2017." AAAP Publications, American
    Academy of Pediatrics, November 2019, https://pediatrics.
    aappublications.org/content/144/5/e20191187.

**5** Prior, Ryan, "1 in 4 Young People Are Reporting Suicidal Thoughts. Here's How to Help," CNN, August 15, 2020, https://www.cnn.com/2020/08/14/health/young-people-suicidal-ideation-wellness/index.html.

**6** Jackson, Amanda, "A Crisis Mental-health Hotline Has Seen an 891% Spike in Calls," CNN, April 10, 2020, https://www.cnn.com/2020/04/10/us/disaster-hotline-call-increase-wellness-trnd/index.html.

**7** Lessard, J. C., & Moretti, M. M, "Suicidal Ideation in an Adolescent Clinical Sample: Attachment Patterns and Clinical Implications," *Journal of Adolescence*, 21, (1998): 383-395.

**8** This term was originally coined by St. John of the Cross in the 16th century.

**9** Goulston, Mark, "Why People Kill themselves, Part 2: It's Not Depression." Medium, June 9, 2018, https://medium.com/@mgoulston/why-people-kill-themselves-its-not-depression-44113406ac79

**10** Legg, Timothy J. Ph.D., PsyD, "Amygdala Hijack: When Emotion Takes Over," Healthline, April 22, 2019, https://www.healthline.com/health/stress/amygdala-hijack.

**11** Favazza, A, *Bodies Under Siege: Self-mutilation and Body Modification in Culture and Society* (2nd ed.) (Baltimore: Johns Hopkins University Press, 1996).

**12** Walsh, B, *Treating Self-injury: A Practical Guide* (New York: Guilford Press, 2005).

**13** Kennedy TM, Ceballo R, "Emotionally Numb: Desensitization to Community Violence Exposure Among Urban Youth," *Development Psychology*, 52(5) (May 2016): 778-89. doi: 10.1037/dev0000112. Epub March 17, 2016, PMID: 26986229.

**14** John 4:4–42

**15**  John 8:3-4

**16**  Erskine, Richard. "Attunement and Involvement: Therapeutic Responses to Relational Needs," 3 (January 1998): 235-244.

**17**  Batterson, Mark, *The Circle Maker: Praying Circles Around Your Biggest Dreams and Greatest Fears* (Zondervan, December 6, 2016).

**18**  Siegal, Daniel J. M.D. and Bryson, Tina Panye Ph.D. *The Power of Showing Up* (New York: Ballantine Books, 2020.)

**19**  American Psychiatric Association, *Diagnostic and Statistical Manual of Mental Disorders* 5th edition (Arlington, VA: Author, 2013).

**20**  "Suicide Claims More Lives than War, Murder, and Natural Disasters Combined," A*merican Foundation for Suicide Prevention,* accessed on February 28, 2020, https://www.theovernight.org/?fuseaction=cms.page&id=1034.

**21**  "Does Depression Increase the Risk for Suicide?" U.S. Department of Health and Human Services, accessed on February 28, 2020, https://www.hhs.gov/answers/mental-health-and-substance-abuse/does-depression-increase-risk-of-suicide/index.html.

**22**  Sommers-Flanagan, J, "Conversations About Suicide: Strategies for Detecting and Assessing Suicide Risk," *Journal of Health Service Psychology,* (2018): 44, 33–45.

**23**  Ribeiro, J. D., Silva, C., & Joiner, T. E, "Overarousal Interacts with a Sense of Fearlessness about Death to Predict Suicide Risk in a Sample of Clinical Outpatients," *Psychiatry Research, 218*(1-2),(2014): 106–112. doi:10.1016/j.psychres.03.036.

**24**  Pennebaker, J. W., Kiecolt-Glaser, J. K., & Glaser, R. "Disclosure of Traumas and Immune Function: Health Implications for Psychotherapy," *Journal of Consulting and Clinical Psychology, 56*(2), (1988): 239–245.

**25** Lieberman MD, Eisenberger NI, Crockett MJ, Tom SM, Pfeifer JH, Way BM. 2007, "Putting Feelings into Words: Affect Labeling Disrupts Amygdala Activity in Response to Affective Stimuli," *Psychological Science*, 5 (May 2007): 421-8. doi: 10.1111/j.1467-9280.2007.01916.x. PMID: 17576282.

**26** Kleinke, C.L., "Gaze and Eye Contact: A Research Review," *Psychological Bulletin*, 100(1), (1986): 78–100.

**27** Hains, S. M. J. & Muir, D. W. "Infant Sensitivity to Adult Eye Direction." *Child Development*, 67, (1996): 1940-1951. doi: 10.2307/1131602

**28** Escalona, S., "Basic Modes of Social Interaction: Their Emergence and Pattering During the First Two Years of Life," *Merrill-Palmer Quarterly of Behavior and Development, 19*(3), (1973): 205-232. Retrieved February 15, 2021 from http://www.jstor.org/stable/23084035

**29** Leong, Victoria & Byrne, Elizabeth & Clackson, Kaili & Georgieva, Stanimira & Lam, Sarah & Wass, Sam, "Speaker Gaze Increases Information Coupling Between Infant and Adult Brains" *PNAS* (November 2017). https://doi.org/10.1073/pnas.1702493114.

**30** Hendrix, Harville. *Getting the Love You Want: A Guide for Couples*. (New York: Henry Holt and Company, 2007).

**31** Vaish, Amrisha et al, "Not All Emotions are Created Equal: The Negativity Bias in Social-emotional Development," *Psychological Bulletin*, vol. 134,3 (2008): 383-403. doi:10.1037/0033-2909.134.3.383

**32** Fredrickson, BL and Losada, MF, "Positive Affect and the Complex Dynamics of Human Flourishing," *American Psychologist*, 60(7) (2005): 678-686. doi:10.1037/0003-066x.60.7.678.

33  Zia, Asbah & Malik, Anila & Masoom Ali, Saima, "Father and Daughter Relationship and Its Impact on Daughter's Self-Esteem and Academic Achievement," *Academic Journal of Interdisciplinary Studies* (2015). 10.5901/mjss.2015.v4n1p311.

34  Pickersgill, Martyn et al. "The Changing Brain: Neuroscience and the Enduring Import of Everyday Experience." *Public Understanding of Science (Bristol, England)* vol. 24,7 (2015): 878-92. doi:10.1177/0963662514521550.

35  Leaf, Caroline, *Switch on Your Brain: The Key to Peak Happiness, Thinking, and Health* (Grand Rapids, MI: Baker Books, 2015).

36  Dusek JA, Otu HH, Wohlhueter AL, Bhasin M, Zerbini LF, Joseph MG, Benson H, Liebermann TA, "Genomic Counter-Stress Changes Induced by the Relaxation Response," *PLoS One,* 3(7) (July 2, 2008) e2576.

37  Amen, Daniel G. *Change Your Brain, Change Your Life: The Breakthrough Program for Conquering Anxiety, Depression, Obsessiveness, Anger, and Impulsiveness* (New York: Three Rivers Press, 2000).

38  Tseng, J., Poppenk, J. "Brain Meta-state Transitions Demarcate Thoughts Across Task Contexts Exposing the Mental Noise of Trait Neuroticism." *Nature Communications* 11, 3480 (July 13, 2020). https://doi.org/10.1038/s41467-020-17255-9. https://www.queensu.ca/gazette/media/news-release-queen-s-university-researchers-uncover-brain-based-marker-or-thought-worms-show.

39  Tyng, Chai M et al, "The Influences of Emotion on Learning and Memory," *Frontiers in Psychology,* vol.81454 (August 24, 2017). doi:10.3389/fpsyg.2017.01454.

**40**  Nerurkar A, Bitton A, Davis RB, Phillips RS, Yeh G, "When Physicians Counsel About Stress: Results of a National Study," *JAMA Intern Med,* 173(1) (2013): 76–77. doi:10.1001/2013.jamainternmed. 480.

**41**  Salleh, Mohd Razali, Life Event, Stress and Illness," *The Malaysian Journal of Medical Sciences: MJMS* vol. 15,4 (2008): 9-18.

**42**  Nerurkar, Aditi et al, "When Physicians Counsel About Stress: Results of a National Study," 76-77.

**43**  Miller, F E., "Challenging and Changing Stress-Producing Thinking," *The Western Journal of Medicine,* vol. 174 (2001): 49-50. doi:10.1136/ewjm.174.1.49.

**44**  Ackermann, Courtney E, "CBT's Cognitive Restructuring for Tackling Cognitive Distortions," Positive Psychology, January 6, 2021, https://positivepsychology.com/cbt-cognitive-restructuring-cognitive-distortions.

**45**  Reviewed by Howard A. Paul ABPP Book Review Editor Ph.D, "A Review of: The Worry Cure: Seven Steps to Stop Worry from Stopping You. Robert L. Leahy." *Child and Family Behavior Therapy*, 30:2 (2008): 173-186. doi: 10.1080/07317100802060344.

**46**  Marcus, Aurelius, Martin Hammond and Diskin Clay, *Meditations,* (London: Penguin Classics, 2006).

**47**  Duckworth, Angela, *Grit: The Power of Passion and Perseverance* (New York: Scribner/Simon & Schuster, 2016).

**48**  Masten A, Best K, Garmezy N, "Resilience and Development: Contributions from the Study of Children Who Overcome Adversity," *Development and Psychopathology,* 2 (1990): 425–444.

**49**  Siegel, Daniel J. and Bryson, Tina P. *The Yes Brain: How to Cultivate Courage, Curiosity, and Resilience in Your Child*, First edition (New York: Bantam, 2018).

**50** Souri, Hosein and Hasanirad, Turaj, "Relationship between Resilience, Optimism and Psychological Well-Being in Students of Medicine," *Procedia - Social and Behavioral Sciences*, (December 2011). 30.15411544.10.1016/j. sbspro.2011.10.299.

**51** Seligman, Marty, *Learned Optimism: How to Change Your Mind and Your Life*, (Knopf Doubleday, 2006).

**52** Siegel, Daniel J. and Bryson, Tina, *The Yes Brain*

**53** National Scientific Council on the Developing Child, "Supportive Relationships and Active Skill-Building Strengthen the Foundations of Resilience," Working Paper No. 13 (2015). Retrieved from www.developingchild. harvard.edu

**54** Duckworth, Angela, *Grit*

**55** Siegel, Daniel J. and Tina Payne Bryson, *The Yes Brain.*

**56** Dweck, Carol S., *Mindset: The New Psychology of Success* (New York: Random House, 2006).

**57** Vygotsky, L. S., *Mind in Society: The Development of Higher Psychological Processes* (Cambridge, MA: Harvard University Press, 1978).

**58** Curtin, Sally C. M.A. and Heron, Melonie, Ph.D., "Death Rates Due to Suicide and Homicide Among Persons Aged 10–24: United States, 2000–2017," CDC, National Vital Statistics System, October 2019, https://www.cdc.gov/ nchs/data/databriefs/db352-h.pdf.

**59** John Gottman in his research on emotion coaching. Heard on *Parenting Great Kids with Dr. Meg Meeker Podcast,* Episode 78, April 9, 2019.

**Will Hutcherson** is a national speaker, the founder of Curate Hope, and a Next Gen/Youth pastor of 15 years. Over the past several years, he has become passionate about finding practical ways to bring hope to kids and teens who are facing increasing amounts of anxiety, depression, and despair. This led to him starting Curate Hope, a non-profit that focuses on suicide prevention, mental health awareness, and part-nering with educators and parents to help heal despair in teens. Will seeks to build a bridge between the local church and the schools and families who are navigating this mental health crisis.

Every year, he speaks to thousands of teenagers in public schools across the country, offering a message of hope. In his roles on executive teams at multi-site churches, Will has help train and develop many ministry leaders as well as coach and consult other pastors around the country. He has spoken at events like Orange Conference, Orange Tour, and Florida Business Professionals of America Student Leadership Conference.

He's also been featured on numerous podcasts, including Life. ChurchParents and National Community Church. He lives in the Sunshine State with his wife Arianne and three kids, where you might find him listening to 90's R&B or hunting alligators.

**Dr. Chinwé U. Williams** is a Board-Certified Counselor (NCC), Certified Professional Counselors Supervisor (CPCS) and a Licensed Professional Counselor (LPC) in the state of Georgia. Dr. Williams has worked in the area of counseling for over fifteen years and counselor education and training for ten years. She has served as a college and high school counselor, group facilitator, executive coach, and currently works as a therapist and consultant in schools, non-profit, faith-based, and corporate work settings. Her expertise lies in areas of stress/anxiety management, trauma recovery, intersection of faith and mental health, diversity and inclusion and youth and adult wellness.

Dr. Williams has previously taught at Georgia State University, Argosy University, University of Central Florida, and Rollins College and is a member of Licensed Professional Counselors Association (LPCA) and an active member of the American Counseling Association (ACA).

Dr. Williams is also a published journal author and a frequently featured expert blog and podcast contributor on topics related to child, adolescent, and adult mental health and wellness. She is also a speaker at local, national, and international conferences and the owner and principal therapist at Meaningful Solutions Counseling & Consulting, where she maintains a growing private practice in Roswell, Ga serving adolescents, young adults, individuals, and families.